AF251711

MEDIA PRODUCTION
for Business or Education

by Valentine DelVecchio

Graphic Design By Melody Mullis

REFERENCE DESK BOOKS
MORRO BAY, CALIFORNIA

Acknowledgements

Special thanks to Melody Mullis for graphic design and original illustrations, and to Joyce Kadoch for editorial advice. Thanks also to Tom Imming for his assistance in making this project go smoothly.

Disclaimer

This book is the result of the author's experience and research. Most production techniques are standardized; any similarity between this book and other publications is coincidental and unintentional. Some terms and names used in this book are trademarks and are property of the respective owners.

Media Production for Business or Education

ISBN: 0-9625749-3-7

Printed in the United States of America

Business

Education

Table of Contents
PROD. NO.
TIME
SCENE
TAKE
1
1
DATE   1994
DIRECTOR   DelVecchio
PRODUCED BY   Reference Desk Books

INTRODUCTION

Welcome to basic audiovisual materials and methods. This is a <u>practical</u> book, designed with the real world in mind. Most teachers and business people do not have the time to develop elaborate multi-media showcases for their classes or meetings. Most schools and businesses do not have budgets for elaborate and expensive audiovisual production equipment. Therefore, I will concentrate on the practical, inexpensive, realistic materials that you can actually use in the classroom or the board room. You will learn sophisticated techniques, such as slide/tape production and videotape production, as well as simple items such as teaching pictures. Slide programs will be practical, using only one projector instead of multi-projector techniques. Likewise, only one camera video production, rather than three camera studio production will be discussed. You do not always have to produce your own media. There are many very well produced commercial filmstrips, movies, transparencies, slide programs, and videotapes available. There is also junk! Selection criteria will be discussed throughout the book.

Media production requires efficient design and skillful crafting. School aged youngsters grow up with television, and are used to slick visuals. Likewise, in business, clients expect your best efforts. They will not accept poor quality visuals, or sound, in the classroom or meetings. You will learn that audience analysis, task analysis, and behavioral objectives are required for even the simplest teaching picture. The biggest mistake most novice producers make is lack of design. Do not just throw a slide program together and hope it works. Measure the results of behavioral change to determine learned outcomes, using tests.

You, the producer, are sender of a message; the student or client is the receiver. Carefully select and design the means (medium) of sending that message.

Part 2 of this book is primarily for teachers. It is a teacher's manual and includes lesson plans, and information about the exam, grades, and class attendance. Institutional trainers or business trainers may also want to use Part 2 as a guide for teaching media production to employees.

Some productions require teams, or crews; however, most of the materials can be made by one person. More sophisticated programs, on the other hand, require teamwork. Teamwork is an efficient way for producers with limited time to make quality audiovisual materials.

For clarity and convenience, the word *producer* will be used from now on to mean teacher, trainer, instructor, or presenter. Enjoy the book and have fun with media!

MEDIA SELECTION

What constitutes a good media program? A good product, whether a simple teaching picture or complex video production, will have some basic requirements. These are:

1. The program will whet the appetite for further study on the topic. Avoid "information overload." Ideally, your program should not be loaded with too much content information. A person can only assimilate so much information from media. Provide just enough information to stimulate the viewer to want to learn more about the subject. For example, in a business sales presentation, entice the viewer by giving bottom line profit possibilities for your product. Details of how to get to that bottom line will be learned in follow-up, perhaps with a detailed handout of steps. There is a term for this kind of educational product development; it is called "lean programming." Give only the bare bones essence of the subject. "Fat programming" is heavy production, bloated with too much information. It may dazzle the viewer, but not be retained.

2. Your product will be visually stimulating; keeping the viewer's interest throughout the program. Take full advantage of the medium you are using. For example, if using video, have plenty of motion in the scenes. It is a motion medium. Do not have two people sitting and talking about a subject with the camera on one person for a long time. Keep the visual moving, use pans and zooms, and cut often. Likewise for a slide program. Rapidly pace the program to achieve motion. Do not let slides stay on the screen too long; the viewer tunes out. And please make those overhead transparencies interesting! Nothing bores a viewer as much as the plain typed out, black and white overhead transparency.

3. Good media programs will provide feedback, especially on programs that teach skills. Students need to know how they are doing. You can build feedback into a program, but this usually requires someone present to evaluate progress and give the student suggestions for improvement.

4. The program briefly reviews content. A good product will review highlights of the presentation, usually at the end. Sometimes, especially for longer programs, you will provide review at various points throughout.

Include an assessment test with the product. How do you know the program works? Everyone in the audience seemed really interested, smiles on their faces and lots of questions, they must have learned a lot, right? Wrong! Do not assume they learned anything from your presentation. Make a little quiz testing the student's knowledge of the content after using or viewing the program. This can be done with a control group of viewers, perhaps friends or associates who do not have knowledge of the subject presented. It is not necessary to test every group that uses the program. Each test question will evaluate a specific behavioral objective as stated in the design documents described later.

Part One
Chapter One

Teaching Pictures
Mounting
Lamination
Tracing
Accordian Folds
Bulletin Boards
Audio Tapes
Transparencies
Overlays

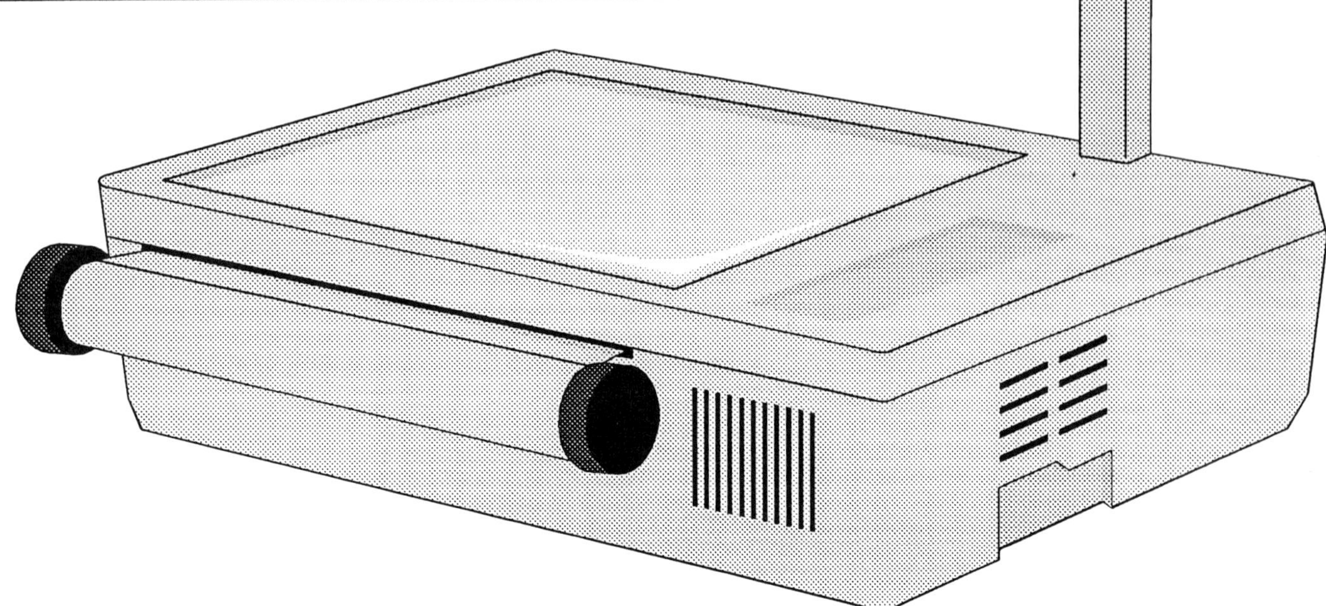

SIMPLE MEDIA

This chapter introduces you to the world of instructional media. Media is the plural of medium. Webster's <u>Dictionary</u> defines the word medium (as it pertains to this book):

"1. a means of effecting or conveying something

2. a channel of communication; esp: a means of disseminating ideas...

3. a mode of artistic expression "

You will learn that instructional media encompass all of the above definitions. A specific medium, video for example, will convey a message that you specifically design. This medium is a channel of communication between teacher and student. It is often a way to creatively or artisticly express an educational concept.

Before you learn how to produce instructional media, you need to know how to design it. Each media product or program must have design documents. The documents consist of the task analysis and description of the target audience. You also need a lesson plan which incorporates goals, activities, and instructional, or behavioral objectives. If you are new at writing lesson plans, take one from this book as a guide.

Objectives provide the backbone of teaching. You can measure learned outcomes by how well the student masters specific objectives. The structure of objectives allows for easy measurement. In order for something to be learned, a behavior needs to be changed. For ease and convenience in writing objectives, we will use the INDOC system to remember and apply behaviors. The university educators who developed this system, concluded that all behaviors can be categorized by the following verbs: Identify, Name, Describe, Order, and Construct. Hence the term INDOC. These terms have many synonyms; for example *label* can be used for name, *demonstrate* for describe, and *list* for order.

Constructing the objective is simple. It has three parts: the conditions, behavior, and performance level.

You set the conditions under which the student will accomplish the objective. It usually starts with the word "Given."

"Given the class lecture..."

Part two is the behavior. Use one of the INDOC terms.

"Given the class lecture, the student will name the first President of United States..."

The last part of the objective is what you consider an acceptable measure of performance.

"Given the class lecture, the student will name the first President of the United States. Acceptable performance consists of the student verbally stating George Washington."

Behavioral objectives can be either the terminal, or final outcome, or a sub-objective. Sometimes we call sub-objectives "enroute objectives" because they are one step toward the final outcome.

Behavioral objectives fall in the cognitive domain, that is applying the mental process of memory, judgement, or reasoning. Affective domain objectives relate to emotional response. Include some affective domain objectives in media design. An example would be "The student will understand the pressures of being the first President of the United States." Notice the verb is more nebulous, and hard to measure. Common verbs in affective domain objectives would be appreciate, enjoy, accept, understand and sympathize.

Task analysis is another aspect of media design. Does the learning require certain tasks? For example, a child learning how to tie his or her shoes must accomplish certain tasks on the way to the end result. The end result becomes the terminal objective and the tasks are the enroute objectives.

Carefully analyze the target population of the media product. If, for example, the product is a slide program, is it for business people or a fifth grade geography class? Each audience is unique and you must know the target of your message. Ask yourself questions such as, is there a wide age range within the audience, a diversity of ethnic backgrounds, are they urban, rural, handicapped, veterans, etc.?

Some media products such as filmstrips, slide programs, and video productions require scripts. We will cover scripting later, but it is part of the design document package.

TEACHING PICTURES

Teaching pictures are a simple medium that can stand alone to teach specific outcomes. Pictures are either photographs or drawn graphics, or a combination of both. Carefully select your visual based on the design documents. Often, you will use mounted pictures from magazines. These are commonly called "tear sheets" because you cut or tear them from an old magazine. This lesson teaches how to mount these pictures, using either wet or dry techniques.

WET MOUNTING A VISUAL

In addition to the visual, you will need a piece of poster board slightly larger than the visual. Also, have a pencil, rubber cement, ruler and scissors or a cutting board. Steps in wet mounting using rubber cement are:

Register the visual on the poster board by placing pencil marks on the opposite corners.

Place rubber cement on one-half of the poster board and one-half of the visual.

Place the cemented half of the visual on the cemented half of the poster board and press lightly.

Place rubber cement on the other half of the poster board. Place rubber cement on the remaining half of the visual.

Lightly press the visual to the poster board.

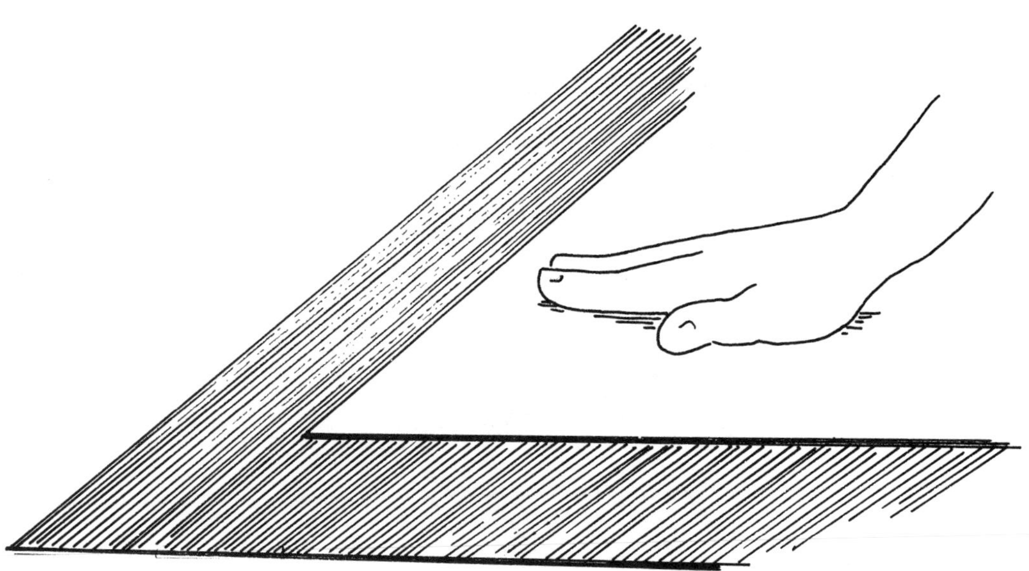

Use a ruler to smooth out the visual on the poster board.

Rub-off the excess rubber cement with a clean finger.

Trim the edges of the visual evenly with scissors or a cutting board.

For dry mounting, in addition to the visual and poster board, you will need dry mounting tissue such as MT-5, a tacking iron, a dry mount press or regular clothes iron, ruler, cutting knife or safety razor blade, and a weight (the weight can be heavy books). Before starting, turn on the dry mount press to 225 degrees and let it preheat. It takes about 5 minutes to heat. Use a permanent press, either nylon or polyester, setting if you are using a clothes iron instead of a press.

Steps in dry mounting:

Rough cut a piece of MT-5 and tack it to the back of the visual with the tacking iron.

Trim the edges of the visual with a ruler and a knife or razor blade.

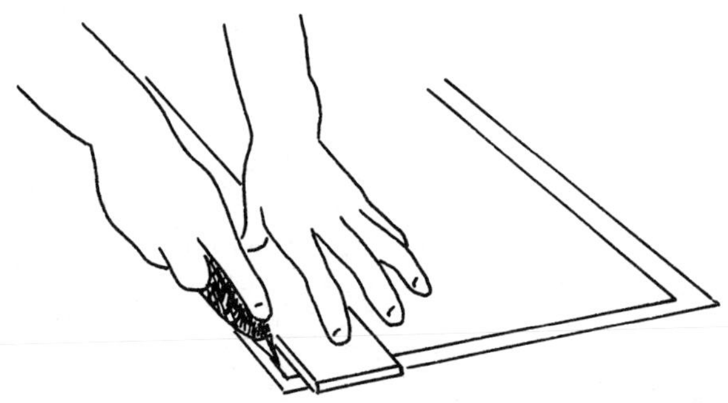

Register the visual and mounting tissue on the poster board using pencil marks on opposite corners.

Tack opposite ends of the loose tissue within the registration marks (be careful to tack just the tissue, not the visual itself).

Place the tacked visual into the dry mount press and heat for about 2 minutes, or iron the visual until it adheres to the poster board.

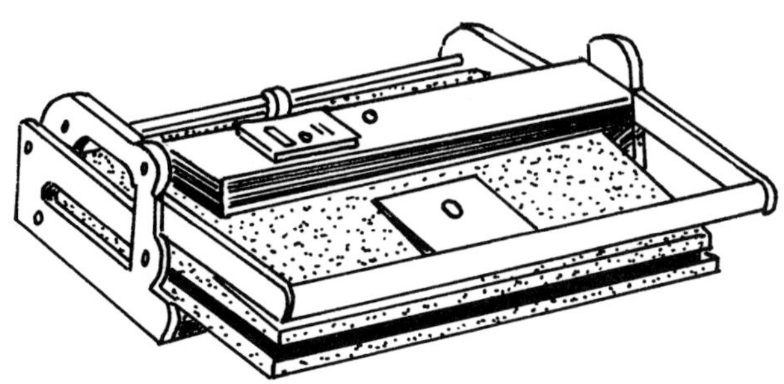

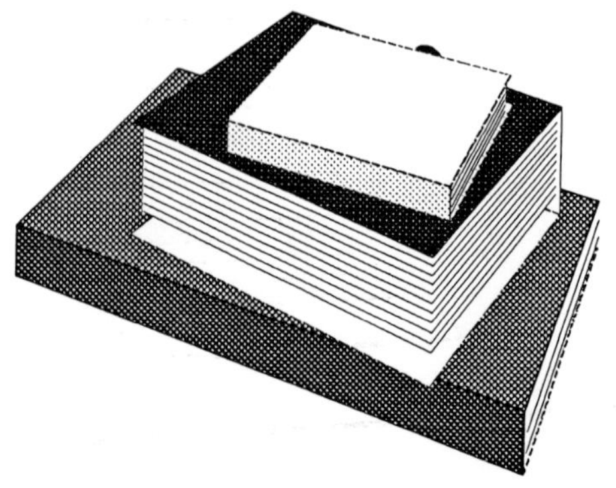

LAMINATING YOUR FINISHED DRY MOUNT

Plastic lamination makes your teaching picture more durable. Do not laminate a wet mounted visual. The heat of the press will melt the glue and you will have a major mess in the press! The most common laminating film is made by Seal, Inc. called Seal-Lamin. Other similar products are available.

First, pre-heat the dry mount press to the temperature required for the material you are using. The temperature will be on the material package, typically 180 degrees.

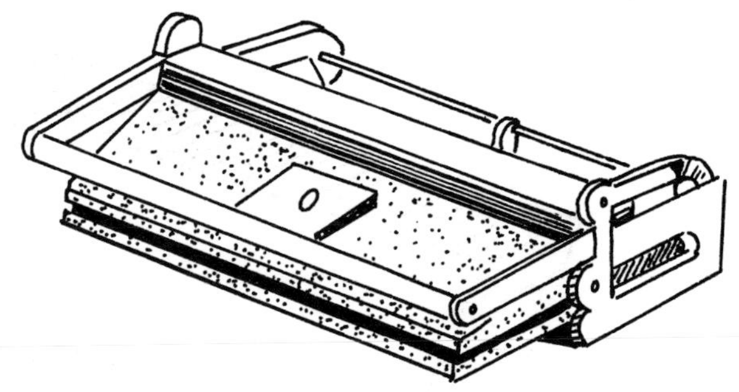

14

While the press is heating to the proper temperature, cut a piece of lamination material slightly larger than the visual.

Fold the excess material over the edges of the visual and tack the film to the back of it with a tacking iron.

Place the visual with the tacked lamination film into the press. Cook for the time recommended by the film manufacturer. The time is usually about 2 minutes. Check the press occasionally.

Once the lamination film is firmly heated onto the visual, (the mount has no bubbles) remove it from the press. Immediately place the laminated visual under a weight. The weight can be a metal plate, books, or any other heavy object. Leave the visual under the weight until it cools so that it will not curl.

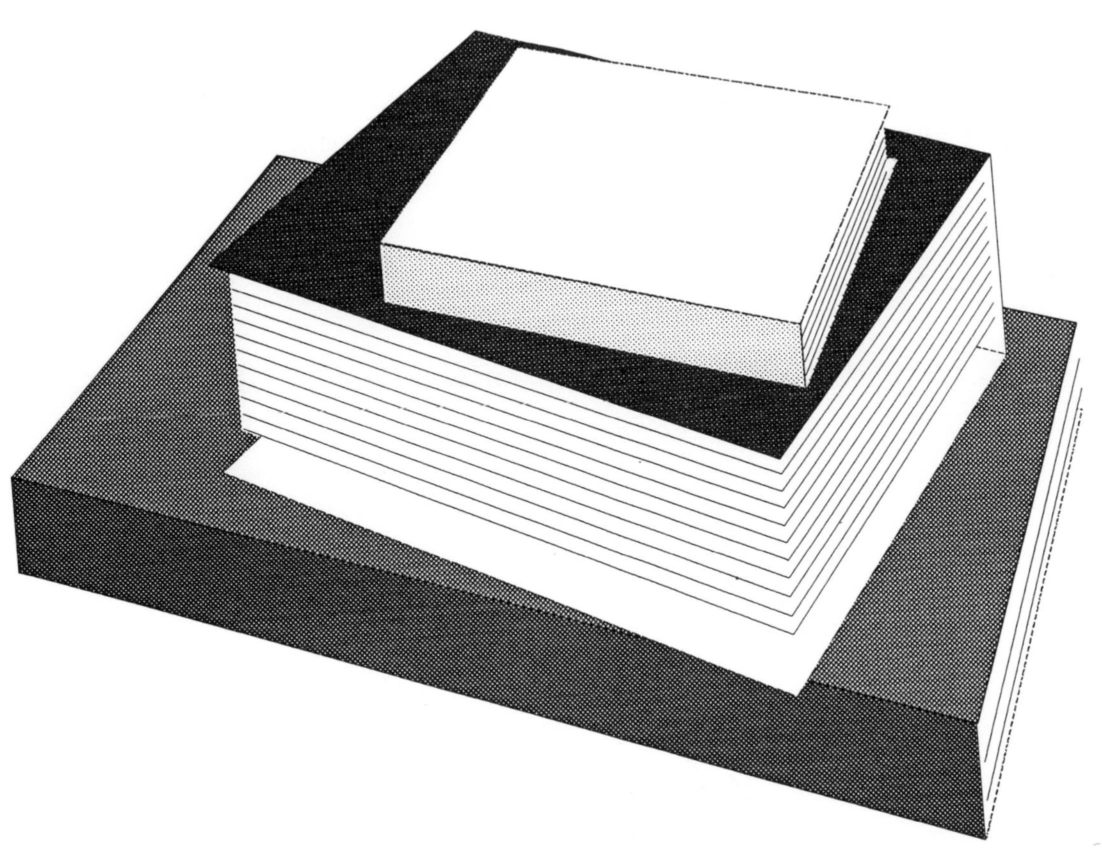

Note that it is not necessary to use a special weight. Large books work just fine. You can also use a regular dry or steam iron in place of the dry mount press and/or tacking iron. Just make sure you do not overheat the iron which could damage the visual or lamination material.

LARGE SIZE VISUALS

Large visuals are useful as presentation aids, teaching pictures, or display and decoration. You do not have to be an artist to make a drawing for a large visual. Enter the tried and true opaque projector. It is the large and noisy clunker, probably shoved in a corner of the AV storeroom. Many people do not like these machines because they are awkward. But, as you will see, they can be very handy.

Opaque projectors are used like overhead projectors; they throw a large image onto a screen or wall. However, they project opaque objects, such as pictures from books or magazines, or real life objects like rocks. Unlike overhead projectors which require transparent film, opaque projectors will project any object.

Tracing the opaque image:

First select something you wish to trace. Make sure it is opaque.

Tape a large piece of poster board, paper, or whatever else you want as a canvas, onto a wall in front of the projector.

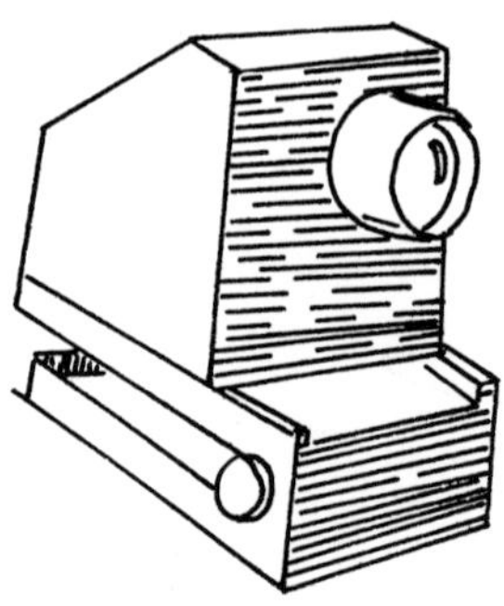

Place the selected item to trace on the tray of the opaque projector and close it. Focus the projected image onto the poster board. You may have to move the projector back or forward to adjust the size of the image on the poster board.

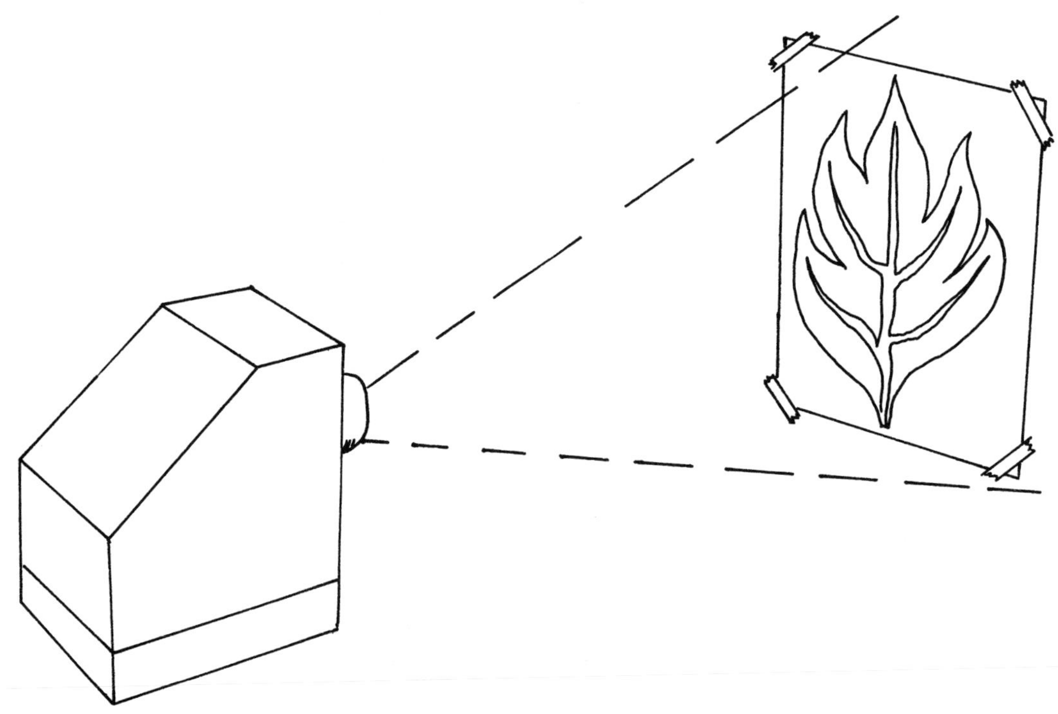

Trace the projected image. It is not necessary to stay within the lines. Be as creative as you want with your drawing.

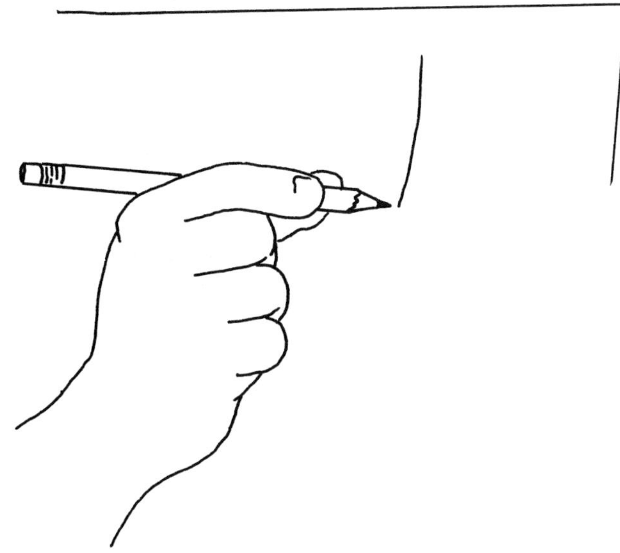

Take down the posterboard once the tracing is finished.

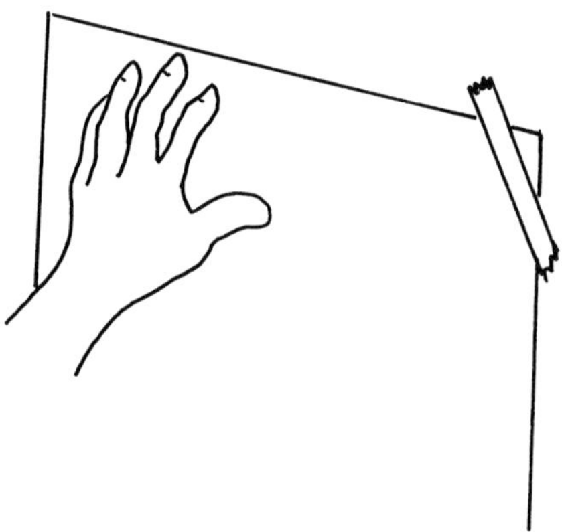

Color the traced image to suit your needs.

ACCORDION FOLDS

An accordion fold is an easy way to present two or more teaching pictures. Simply tape the mounted visuals together on one edge, making an accordion. During presentations, each picture can be unfolded singly, or the fold can be displayed all at once. This medium is good for elementary school classes. It can also be used in business demonstrations in lieu of a flip chart, or for display during a seminar or meeting.

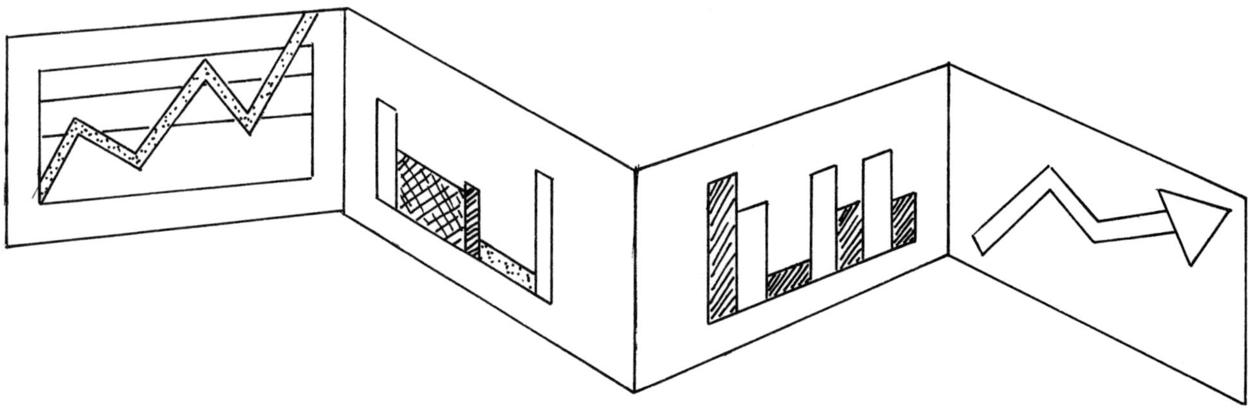

BULLETIN BOARDS

The bulletin board described here is primarily for elementary school use, however, business people may find it useful as a supplement to other presentations. This is most useful when you teach a sequence of actions. Note: if you have access to a cork bulletin board, substitute the sandpaper step with pins.

First, construct the board by gluing felt onto a piece of plywood, or heavy weight posterboard. Your school or business may already have a bulletin board; if so, eliminate this step.

Cut out visuals from drawings, magazine photos, etc. You have the option to dry mount and laminate the cut-out visuals to give them added strength and durability. Follow the steps previously described for mounting and laminating.

Cut sandpaper into small strips; make sure they are smaller than the visuals.

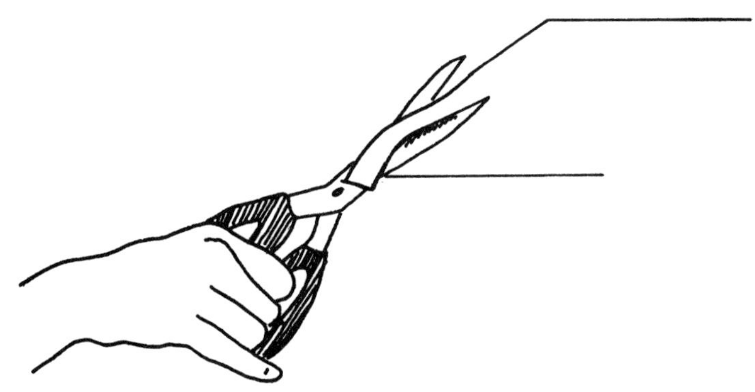

Glue the sandpaper, rough side out, to the visuals. Any mounting and laminating should be done before you affix the sandpaper.

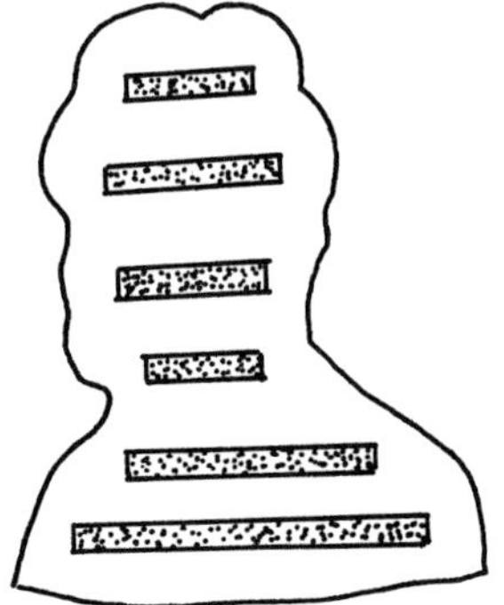

OVERHEAD TRANSPARENCIES

The overhead projector is the most commonly used piece of AV equipment in the
business world. Just about every seminar or presentation includes overhead transparencies. School teachers, especially high school and college, use the overhead frequently.

It is my opinion that the overhead projector is the most misused piece of AV equipment.
Originally designed as an illuminated blackboard, it has become the centerpiece of most
presentations. Unfortunately, most homemade transparencies are awful. They are merely
outlines, or words that the speaker points to while talking. It is not good to be talking
while the audience is trying to read material presented in front of them. The projectors
are often left on for most of the program, usually with the room lights out. What a great
way to put sleeping pill manufacturers out of business! The overhead was designed to be
used with the room lights on, so people can take notes.

Make transparencies colorful and interesting. Design them well, or you will lose the
audience.

22

The easiest way to make transparencies is on a photocopy machine. Many companies make transparency film which works like any copy paper. Simply put your master in the machine and make a copy.

Many schools and businesses have access to a special transparency making machine. 3M makes one called a Thermafax. It makes transparencies the old way, but is still very effective.

This machine uses a heat process to transfer carbon based copies, like those from a copy machine, onto thin transparency film. Transparency films also come in a variety of colors. The most effective way to make color transparencies is to produce black and white outlines with the Thermafax, then color the transparency later.

Thermal process:

First, photocopy your material.

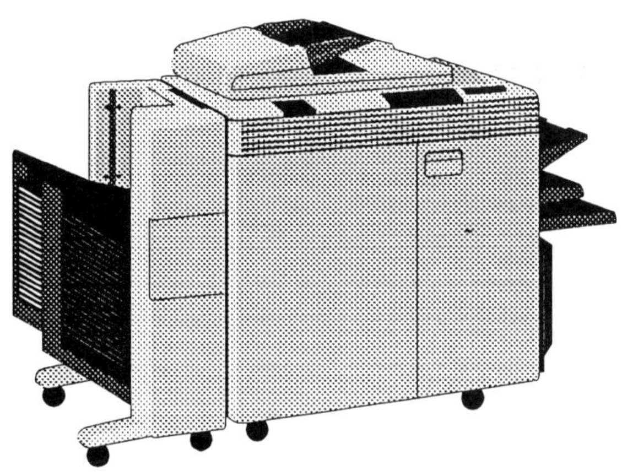

Set the Thermafax to the desired darkness level.

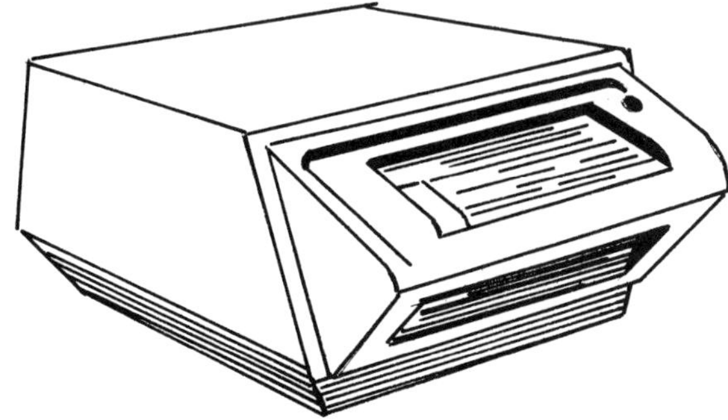

Place your photocopy on a piece of blank transparency film, and put the pack through the Thermafax. Check the directions on the box of transparency film to determine exactly how to place the photocopy. Different brands require different positioning.

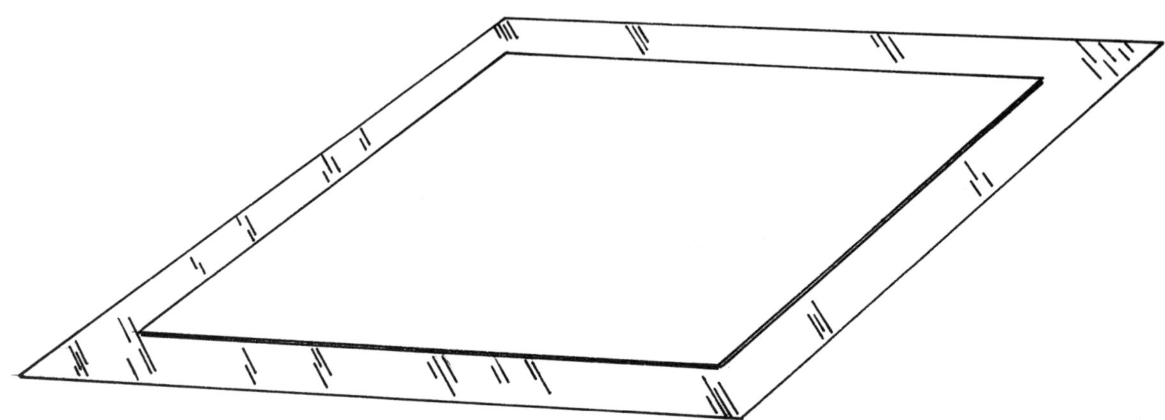

Color the transparency as desired. Use a dark pen with permanent ink, such as a Sharpie brand. Regular felt pens tend to be too light, and can also rub off.

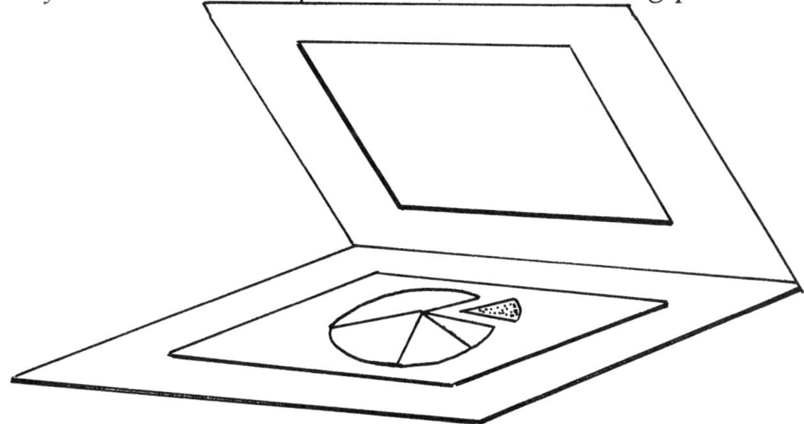

If you do not have access to either a thermafax or a copy machine, then draw images on
clear acetate.

Usually lights are left on in the classroom when viewing overhead transparencies, so for
optimum results, use dark letters on light or clear backgrounds. This scheme makes the
best image contrast for adequate viewing.

OVERLAY TRANSPARENCIES

Individual transparencies can be combined into overlays. Overlays are very useful in
classroom teaching and business presentations. Planning is important for every individual
transparency when making an overlay. Remember that each successive transparency
should contain new information to superimpose over the previous.

Make the individual transparencies as described above.

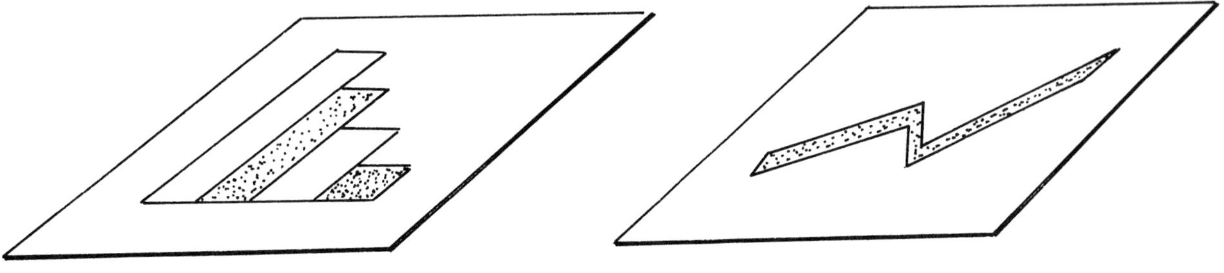

Mount the base transparency onto a cardboard frame.

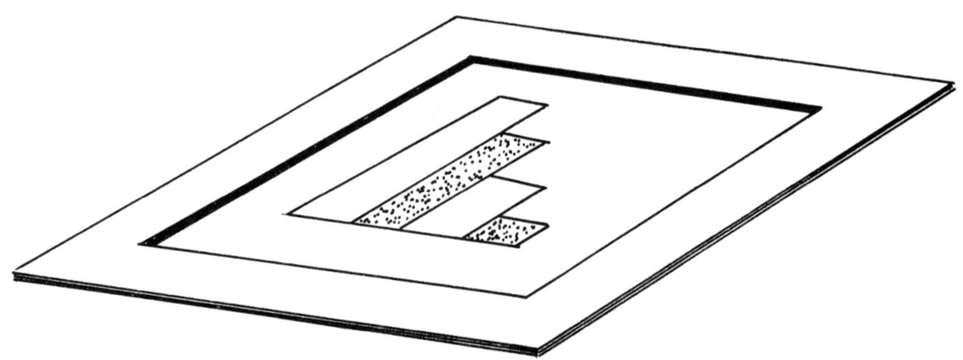

Use masking tape to mount the second transparency to the frame.

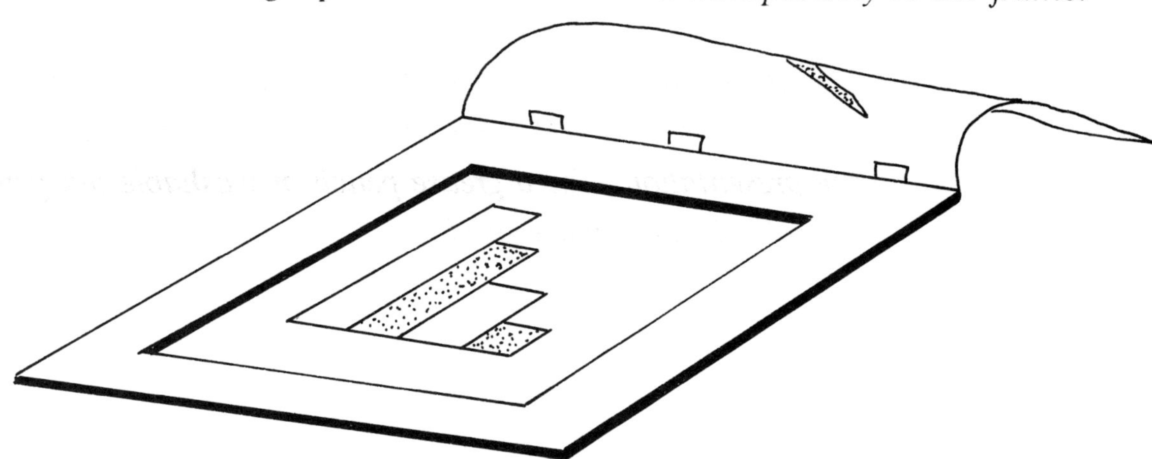

Mount subsequent transparencies as required. Do not tape two transparencies on the same edge, or you will not be able to overlay them. Tape each transparency onto a different side of the cardboard frame.

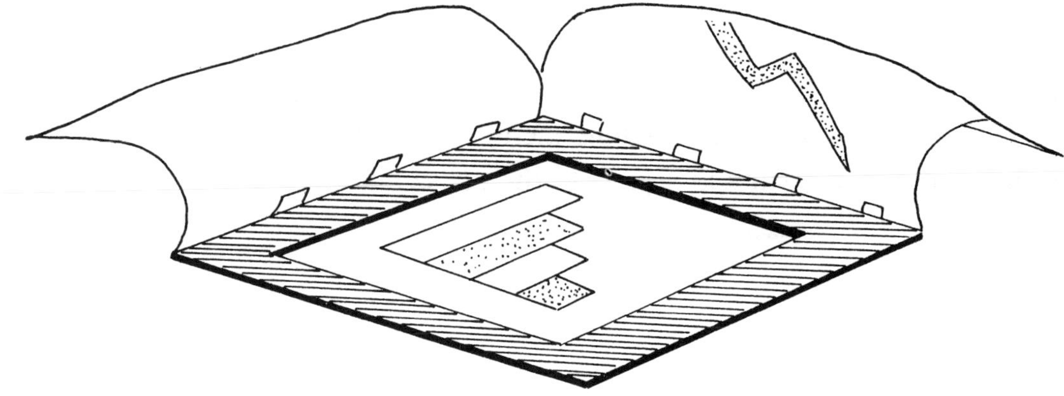

You can also use a grease pencil to write on the transparency. It is easily removed with tissue. Use a pencil or special pointer directly on the transparency when highlighting while projected. Do not point to the projected image on the screen; you will get in the way or the pointer may cast a shadow on the image.

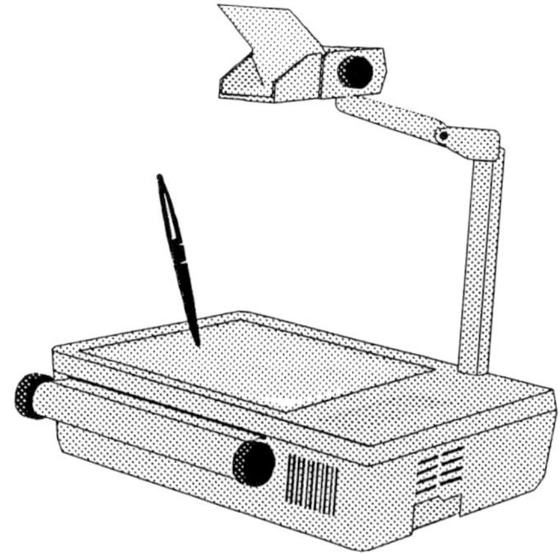

Some overhead projectors have roller mounts to allow you to use a roll of clear acetate. This enables you to write, making your transparency as you go along during the presentation. Use a grease pencil or washable ink pen so the roll can be easily cleaned and reused.

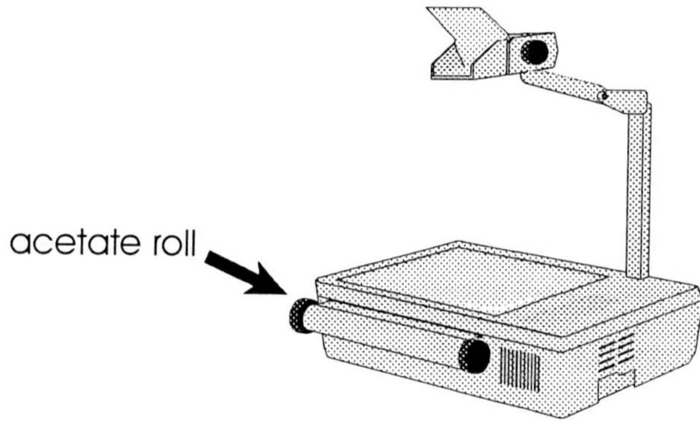

Remember, do not overuse or abuse the overhead projector. Use a blackboard, flip chart, accordion fold, or other teaching picture in addition to, or instead of, the overhead projector. These will add variety to the presentation.

AUDIO TAPE PRODUCTION

Audio tape instruction is still viable in this day of visual images. Many companies produce instructional audio tapes on everything from how to reduce stress, to learning a new language. Quality of blank tape is consistently high among the name brand manufacturers. New technology, such at Digital Audio Tape (DAT), brings superior digital sound quality to audio tape.

Audio tapes are also used in synchronization with slide presentations, as you will learn later. The basic recording techniques, except for the synchronization part, are the same for both uses of audio tape.

Good instructional audio tapes start with good scripts. Carefully construct a script based on your behavioral objectives. Keep the script lean, that is keep it free of unnecessary narrative. Another tip is to use two or more voices for the instruction, preferably male and female. This variation helps keep the listener interested in the program.

Set up your recorder and microphone so that you can comfortably use the controls. Always use a microphone stand so that your hands are free to operate the recorder controls, etc. If possible, have an assistant operate the recorder so you can concentrate solely on reading the script. The ideal way to record is on a reel-to-reel machine. The quality is so much better, and there is no noise from the motor, or tape hiss. It is also easier to back up and record over mistakes on a reel-to-reel machine.

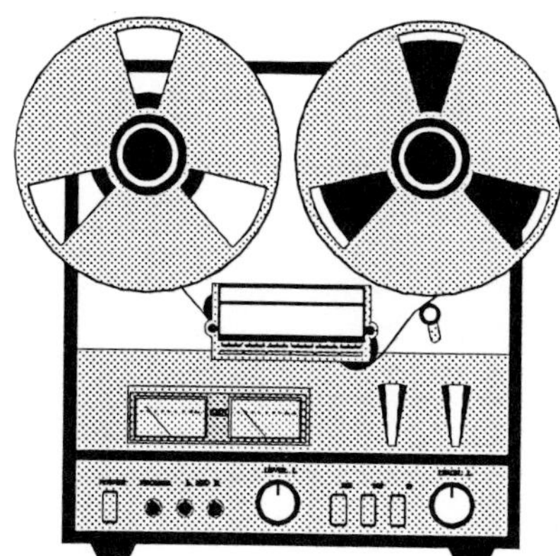

The final product can then be dubbed onto cassette tape. But let us assume you do not have access to the reel-to-reel recorder, nor the time. Cassette machines record at slower speeds and consequently have a slightly audible hiss. This can be eliminated by using a machine with noise reduction, or an equalizer. The hiss, however, is not always a problem and you may find it easy to live with. Most small cassette recorders do very well with voice (better than music, for example).

Most cassette recorders have built-in condenser microphones which may work well for your situation. I recommend, however, that you use a separate stand alone microphone and stand. The separate microphone can be either the multidirectional or unidirectional type.

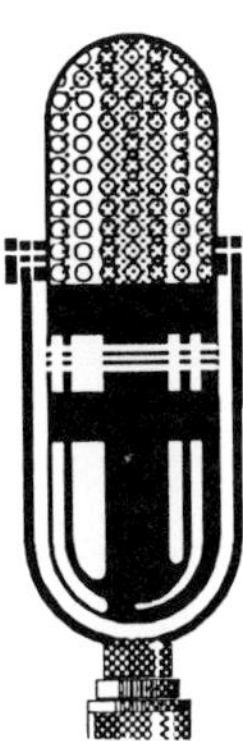

Whichever system you use, the key is how you read the script. Make it interesting. Use voice inflection on the words you wish to emphasize. One tip is to maintain voice strength at the end of sentences. It is common for most of us to drop or lower our voices at the end of sentences. Another tip is to lay out the script pages on a desk or table so that you do not have to flip the pages. Most microphones are sensitive enough to pick-up and record the page turning sounds. Make sure you have individual parts marked on the script if more than one reader is used. You must organize the script so that readers are not bumping into each other while searching for their lines on the pages.

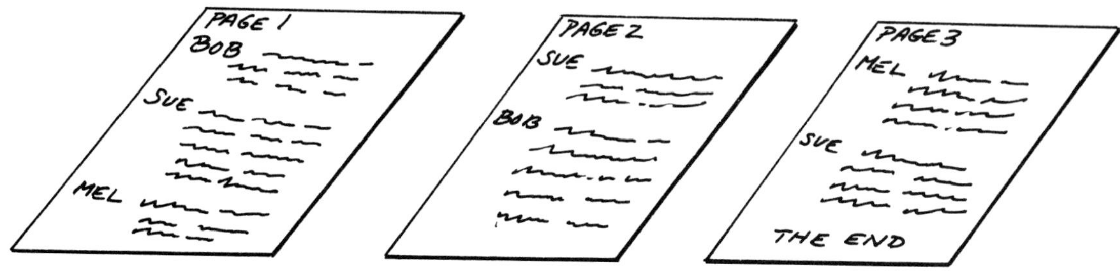

Playback of the finished product is as important as the recording. Use the proper equipment for the audience size. For example, use a more powerful playback machine and bigger speakers for large rooms. These machines provide a cleaner sound at higher volumes. The small portable playback machines are adequate for small groups or classrooms.

You will learn how to synchronize audio tapes with slides in the next lesson.

Chapter Two
PHOTOGRAPHIC MEDIA

Filmstrips
Movies
Slide/Tape Presentations
Video Production

PHOTOGRAPHIC MEDIA

This chapter introduces you to the various types of photographic media. You will also learn how to make a slide/tape program. You learned about simple teaching pictures using tear sheets and drawings in the first chapter. Now, we will get more sophisticated.

FILMSTRIPS

Filmstrips are a staple AV item in schools. There are many fine commercially produced filmstrips. Although appropriate for schools, I do not recommend them for business presentations due to the fact that they are not easily upgraded, so the latest trend cannot be readily incorporated into a business or marketing related filmstrip. There are other limitations, even for classroom use. One limitation is that filmstrips require a special projector. Most schools, however, seem to have one or more. Another limitation is that unless the photography and/or animation is really good, they tend to be boring, especially to young students with short attention spans. Another drawback, albeit common to all photographic media, is that the pictures fade over time. Combine a boring topic with faded visuals and you can imagine the results. Also, a special half-frame 35mm camera is needed to take filmstrip pictures. These cameras are hard to find, I recommend using commercial products instead of making your own. I have learned over the years that filmstrips are more effective if used with small groups of 3 to 5 people, or for individual study.

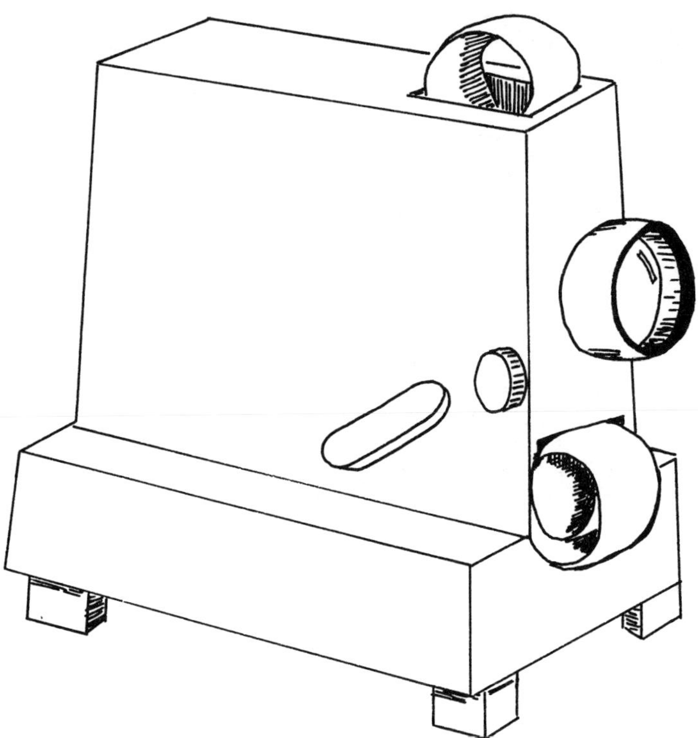

MOVIES

Movies are still heavily used in the classroom and in some board rooms. They are usually 16mm format. Still a viable instructional form, most commercially produced films are excellent. Also, projection equipment is getting simpler to use. Teachers used to dread trying to thread 16mm movies through the projectors. The modern self-threaders are as durable as they are simple; so do not hesitate to use 16mm movies with your instruction. These are still preferred where large audiences need to view a large screen.

The smaller 8mm movies, as well as the" Super 8" format, are still around in limited quantity. The quality varies, depending on age of the film. It is susceptible to fading, scratching, and attracting dirt and dust (so is 16mm film, but that is easier to clean and repair). It is hard to find 8mm movie projectors, so I recommend avoiding this medium unless there is some unique need to use it; a special old home movie for example. These movies can be transferred to video for both archival use and ease of playback. Some high school and college cinematography (the study of film making) classes still use 8mm film because it is more readily available and less expensive than 16mm film stock.

VIDEOTAPE

Video replaced 8mm film as the home movie medium. It also greatly eroded the instructional 16mm film market. Most instructional films are now commercially available on video. Video is more suited to smaller audiences due to the relatively small picture playback size. Unless you are fortunate enough to have access to a large screen television, or a video projection system, video instruction should be used with small to medium (25 or less people) groups. The general rule of thumb is that the projection distance in feet is equal to the size of the screen. For example, a 27-inch monitor is effectively used in rooms no more that 27 feet long. The audience should not be more that 19 feet away from a 19-inch video screen, etc. This same rule of thumb applies to movie projection as well as video. You will learn how to produce simple video programs "in-house," later. Effectively increase the audience capacity for video by adding more screens. It is easy to connect multiple monitors or television sets to the same video recorder by using a signal splitter.

STILL PHOTOGRAPHS

Still photographs are also a usable instructional medium. Remember the opaque projector discussed earlier? Use it to project photographs. A word of warning, do not leave a photograph in an opaque projector for too long, it may burn.

SLIDE/TAPE PRESENTATIONS

Slides combined with audio tape programs are very versatile. They are suitable for both the classroom and the board room. There are many good commercially produced slide programs, but you can easily make one to suit your specific instructional objectives. Let us go through the production process.

1. Planning, as with all instructional media, is essential. Do a task analysis to determine what behavioral objectives to formulate. Slide programs are especially useful in sequential teaching, where one skill builds on another. Write your design documents, to include the terminal and enroute objectives which form the basis for the script.

2. Script your program, using one line of narration for each slide. Slides should not be in view for more than three or four seconds. You can use more than one slide to illustrate longer narration. The time limitation gives the program a brisk pace which keeps audience attention better than slow moving programs. Divide your script pages into two sections, one side for narration, the other for visual. Do either a thumbnail sketch, or be very descriptive about the visual illustrating the narration. A sample script follows.

<u>SLIDE</u>	<u>NARRATION</u>
1. Title	Music
2. Long shot of beach	On those warm summer days...
3. Medium shot of sunbather with soda can	Refresh yourself with Brand X cola...
4. Close-up shot of person drinking soda	... the thirst quencher
5. Close-up shot of brand logo	Music
6. Long shot of beach, fade out	Music

3. Take the required photographs based on the script description. You can also have a professional take the pictures if necessary. Use light colored letters on a dark background when making title or text slides. This scheme makes the best use of the chrome film's contrast.

4. Make the accompanying audio tape as described in the previous section.

5. Synchronize the slides to the tape, using one of the specially designed recorders. Follow the instructions with the recorder. Usually, synchronization requires nothing more than pressing a button on the recorder which records an inaudible sound on the tape. This cue will automatically advance the slides on playback. Some systems can also place an audible tone on the tape. The presenter can manually advance the slide at the tone.

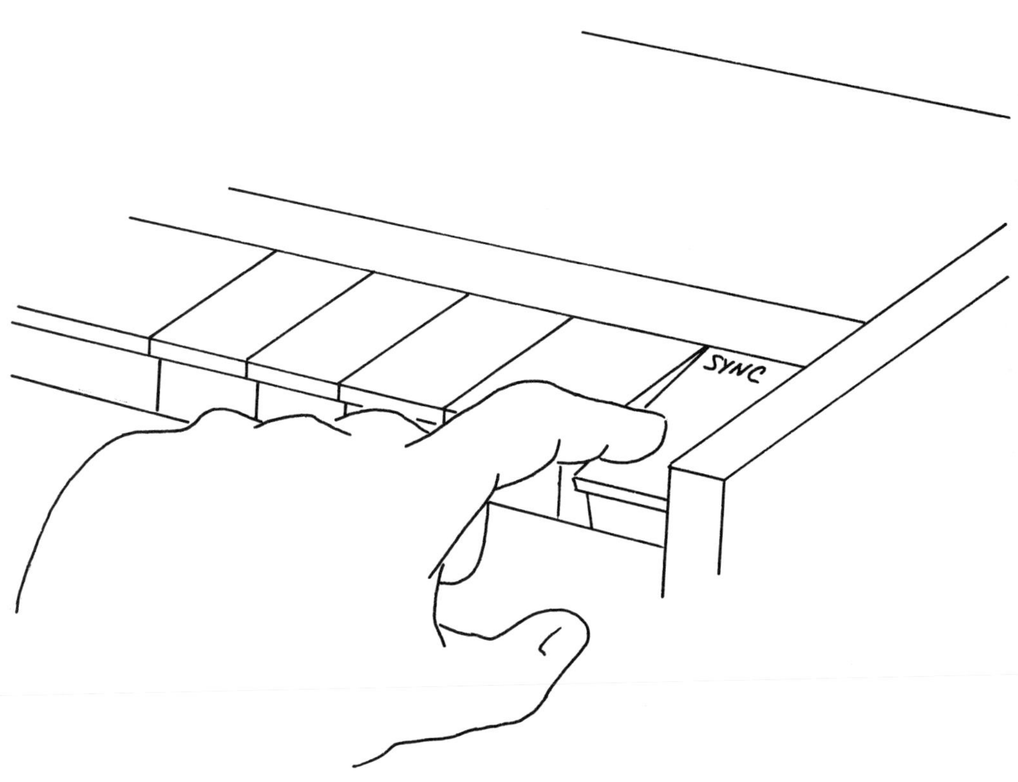

Computer Presentations

Presentation software for IBM, Amiga and MacIntosh computers are capable of making slide programs. Learning curves are steep for most of the available programs and most software is expensive. More hardware is necessary to project the finished product if used in a classroom setting. You may also need a scanner to input photos, otherwise you are limited to charts, graphs, or other computer generated art work. A program of just charts and graphs can indeed be very boring. Photographs are an important aspect of slide programs, and for the most part they are missing from computer generated presentations. According to some computer magazine articles, presentation software has not been widely accepted because of these limitations.

Many computer programs are available, each with strengths and weaknesses. Rather than discuss each program, I will summarize the main features common to all. An outline function allows you to put your main concepts as headings and captions to graphics. Use the outline feature to develop a script. Main headings will become terminal objectives and sub-headings will be enroute objectives. Most programs allow you to generate an outline, or script, with your favorite word processing program, and import it to the presentation program. Whichever method you prefer, the presentation programs have a standard, or default presentation style and color scheme. These styles are geared for a business presentation and can save you formatting time. Creative users can manually develop a more interesting presentation. For example, instead of the standard presentation sequence of fancy title slide, 2 or 3 information slides, 1 summary slide, 2 or 3 more information slides, etc. you can put 2 or 3 flashy attention getting slides together, omit summary slides, etc.

Additionally, presentation programs give you layout options. Usually more than one layout can be used for each slide. You can let the computer design each slide according to default layouts and/or your own prescribed slide layout. Using the standard program color schemes and layouts will give consistency to the final product, however, it may be visually boring to the viewer.

Computer presentation programs are good at building content in slides. The better programs allow you to manage the builds and also have default management. Your bulleted items in the outline will become main titles on a slide; you build from there. Subheadings in the outline can become bulleted subtitles on the slide. You can add, or build, a new subtitle to successive slides creating transition. The smooth dissolve transition created by the presentation software enhances viewer interest in the content. This same technique is much harder to achieve using the manual method, primarily because it takes a second or two for the slides to change in the projector.

Pacing is important with slide programs, whether computer generated or manually produced. Slides should appear for only a few seconds. This keeps the pace fast and the interest high. Do not say more than a line or two of narration for each slide. Humans can absorb both visual and aural messages at one time, so it is not necessary to state verbally what a slide shows visually. Script the program so that you narrate messages related to the visual.

A tip for graphics is to use fonts sparingly. Do not go overboard with lettering styles in each slide. Use one font, preferably a sans serif, or bold style. You can use different colors, rather than different fonts, to highlight selected points in each slide.

 Another weakness of computer generated slide programs is the lack of accompanied narration. Most users of these programs do live narration during the presentation. Although this may be adequate for a business presentation, it hampers individual instruction in an educational setting. In other words, a student cannot use many computer generated slide programs as self-paced individual instruction. Other technologies, specifically CD-I (interactive compact disk) programs, are better suited for self-paced individual instruction on the computer.

Music can be added to computer generated slide programs as you go along, using a computer MIDI (Musical Instrument Digital Interface). This is unlike manual programs which require music to be produced at a different time and then synchronized afterward.

Manually produced slide programs are projected onto a screen by a slide projector, while computer generated programs need a special projector to accomplish the same thing. This is an additional expense, however, many of these units also project videotapes onto a large classroom screen. Computer generated programs have the advantage of projecting the final program on the smaller computer monitor, which may be sufficient for small group training.

One advantage of computer generated slide programs is the ability to make paper copies of the slides. Useful handouts can be produced in this way which would supplement the visual presentation. These pages can also be made into overhead transparencies.

VIDEOTAPE PRODUCTION

Videotape is a useful and versatile medium for instruction. Productions can be simple or complex, based on the instructional needs. My recommendation is to keep production as simple as possible. The time spent on each production will vary. As a general rule, you will spend about one hour of work for every minute of final product. Therefore, a five minute tape would take about five hours to produce. That five hours of work would include pre-production, shooting, and post production. We will discuss each of these at length.

PRE-PRODUCTION AND TAPE FORMATS

Pre-production is the planning and organization of your instructional tape. Planning for video starts the same way as for other media, with instructional objectives. Write the script based on these objectives, and then make a sequence of thumbnail sketches into a storyboard. This is the visual guide for your production. All of these items will become the design documents package.

Videotape is unique because of its various formats. You must decide in pre-production what format tape you will use. This decision may already be made for you if your school or business has equipment. You must use what you have, unless you are fortunate enough to have the budget to rent other, more professional equipment. Let us briefly discuss the formats you will most likely have available to you. Keep in mind that the numbers represent the width of the tape in inches or millimeters.

The standard institutional and industrial format for many years was 3/4 inch tape. It is still popular worldwide, and also used to make master recordings of digital music for compact disk production. Given the right equipment, and the time, this format yields excellent results and is easy to edit. It is gradually becoming the dinosaur of video because of the good quality and high resolution smaller formats. As of this writing, only one company, Sony, makes 3/4 inch equipment. Equipment is expensive and bulky. Tapes are expensive and large, with limited running time; usually 20, 30, or 60 minutes. If you have access to this equipment and someone who can record and edit it, use it!

The most popular tapes today are the two 1/2 inch formats, VHS and BETA. Within those formats are high resolution versions called S-VHS (super VHS) and ED BETA (extended definition BETA). You are probably familiar with the battle between VHS and BETA. VHS won, although BETA has a better picture. Fortunately, BETA is still alive, albeit in less quantity and harder to find. Each format allows you to record at various speeds, thus yielding more recording time per tape. The standard two hour VHS tape (120) can also be recorded at four or six hours. Picture quality decreases as you increase recording time. I strongly recommend you stay with the standard two hour recording. Fortunately, modern camcorders only record in the standard two hour speed. Although I like BETA very much, from here on the term 1/2 inch refers to VHS because of its wider availability. VHS tape is durable, inexpensive and comes in various quality levels. Use the highest quality tape that you can afford. High quality tapes are typically only one or two dollars more than standard tapes.

There is a compact VHS format called VHS-C, which gives the advantage of a small cassette. This could be handy for certain shooting situations when you cannot lug heavy equipment around. The disadvantage of this format is the short recording time, 20 minutes. You can record at a slower speed, however, this yields poor quality as mentioned above. The blank tape is also expensive and you need a special adapter to play in standard VHS machines.

A newer tape size, 8mm, solves the problem of compactness versus recording time. This small tape allows 2 hours of recording time at standard play. The 8mm videocassette is about the size of an audiocassette. You can understand the convenience of this small size. Tapes can fit into your pocket and the picture quality is equal to or better than VHS. This small tape also has more audio versatility than VHS because of the way the tracks are designed. Some people do not understand that you can easily playback an 8mm recording on your regular TV; simply connect the camcorder to the television and play. The camcorder becomes a playback deck. But 8mm is not without its problems. For instance, the small tape size makes it susceptible to dropouts, those small spots on the screen. Static electricity and other factors cause the tape to attract dirt and dust, even in a plastic cassette shell. This happens to all tape formats, but because 8mm is about half the size of VHS, these dust or dirt spots are more evident. Also, 8mm generally does not hold up to much editing, due to the thinness of the tape. The constant movement back and forth of the tape during editing can cause more dropouts, or damage the tape. The problem can be avoided, however, by careful planning and "in-camera editing," which I always recommend no matter which format you use. If compactness and quality are important factors in a camcorder, you should seriously consider the 8mm format.

As mentioned earlier, all of these formats have a high resolution version, which yields better picture sharpness. This increase in sharpness can be useful when editing.The image quality will remain good through a few generations. Each time you make a copy of a tape, or edit onto another tape, it is called a generation. For example, the recorded footage is called first generation. When you take out the bad parts, edit this original footage, it is assembled onto a master, or second generation tape. When you add titles or music tracks, you record those onto another tape, or third generation. Any copies of this would be the fourth generation, as so on. Your good looking original footage can sometimes look bad into the third or fourth generations. So it behooves you to start with the best tape possible to reduce this degradation. If you have access to super VHS (S-VHS)or high 8mm (Hi8), use it. Let us assume, however, that you have a standard VHS camcorder, the common equipment in most schools and businesses.

PRE-PRODUCTION PLANNING

Step 1. Prepare design documents as you would for any educational product.

Step 2. Write the script based on the program goals and the desired instructional objectives stated in your planning documents.

Script writing for video is similar to writing for slide programs. You first must decide how the program is to be presented to the viewer. For example, will there be an on camera host or teacher, or will you be doing voice over the visuals? Will you use a professional cast, groups of students, graphics, etc.? My recommendation is to keep production simple. Write the script succinctly. The following examples show how to match script, or narration, to specific instructional objectives stated in the program design:

<u>Objective</u>

Given the video presentation, the student will name three ways to merchandise the company product in retail stores.

<u>Narration</u>

"There are many ways to make our product more visible to the customer. Place it close to the cash register so they can read the label as they wait in the check-out line. Another way is to put them in a revolving rack by the door, so customers can see them on the way in and out. You can also display them in the store window, or on one of the counters."

Step 3, The Storyboard, takes this process further. Draw small sketches of the visuals to go with the corresponding narration. You can do this many ways. The most common is to make sketches on small pieces of paper with the narration typed below the sketch. These individual pieces can be taped to a board. The advantage of this method is that you can rearrange or edit the shot sequence simply by moving the sketches around the board. Another method is to divide the script sheet into two columns and sketch the visual next to the corresponding narration. This is similar to the method used for slide programs. The advantage is the script and story board are in one compact document. The disadvantage is if you need to reorganize the shot sequence, you have to make a new document.

Here is how the above example would look using the most common method of story boarding:

Notice the abbreviations which identify the type of shot used; they are described later.

42

Production occurs AFTER planning, not vice versa. Good planning will make production more efficient. Follow the sequence of the storyboard. Rehearse scenes so that no mistakes will be made. Mistakes have to be edited out of the tape. Shooting everything in sequence with no mistakes is called "in-camera editing." Use the technique all the time.

Equipment needed for production varies with each program. Keep equipment to a minimum, using at least the following:

1. A camcorder or camera is obviously necessary to take the pictures. From now on I will use the term camera to mean either.

2. A tripod is required to steady the camera. Do not attempt to hold the camera by hand. Your finger movement, breathing, and general shaking will make the picture look bad. I am sure you have all seen those awful home movies with the camera shaking enough to make you seasick.

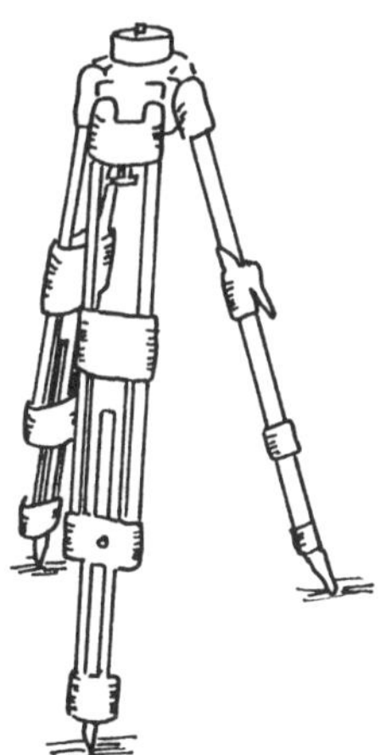

3. At least one video light is necessary to make the picture sharper and more colorful. Even cameras that can shoot in low light will benefit from supplemental lighting. You can use the lights that attach to the camera, or a stand-alone light. Lighting is an art, but you will learn very quickly what looks good and what does not by trial and error. Generally, you will place lights to fill or flood an area. Video lights mounted on the camera do a nice job of this. The only drawback is they are battery powered, and the batteries do not last long; about 20 minutes of continuous light. Many people have one or more back-up batteries for both the video light and the camera.

4. Accessories such as extension cords, extra batteries, etc. are often useful.

Now that you are armed with the right equipment, you need to know what to do. Briefly, I will describe the different types of video shots and how they are used.

There are three basic shots, long, medium and close-up. They are self-explanatory, but each has a specific purpose.

Long shots (LS) are mostly used to establish a scene. The long shot is often called the "establishing shot." Also use the long shot to re-establish the scene, if necessary.

Medium shots (MS) are the most common because of the range of possibilities. They can be used to cover two or more people talking, or other scenes where detail needs to be shown.

Close up (CU) shots are used frequently to show the reaction and response of one person to the previous dialogue or event. They can also be very effective in showing the details of products or objects being promoted. Sometimes a very close shot, called an *extreme close up* (XCU) is used as an effect. For example, showing just the mouth of a person speaking. Do not use XCU shots too much; once or twice in a program can be effective, otherwise the effect becomes trite.

Reaction shots are use to show a person's immediate response, either facial or verbal, to the previous action or narrative. The close-up is most commonly used for reaction shots; however, medium shots can also be effective.

The best productions have a good mix of all the above shots. Start with a long shot to establish the scene and move to medium and close up shots. Carefully plan these to control impact on the viewer.

CAMERA MOVEMENT TECHNIQUES

Camera techniques such as pan, zoom and tilt are commonly used in video production.

The *pan* is horizontal movement of the camera. It can be from left to right or right to left. If you are showing a group of products on a table for instance, do a close up pan as they are described. Do not pan either too fast or too slowly. It takes some practice to judge the best speed of the pan shot.

You "*zoom in*" or "*zoom out*" whenever the camera moves closer or further away from a subject. For example, you can start with a medium shot of a person making a presentation and zoom in to a close-up shot of the face while he or she is speaking. Zoom shots can be on the slow side, but not so slow that the viewer gets impatient. Do not make the zoom too fast, however. Like the pan shot, zooming takes practice.

A *tilt* is when the camera moves up and down a stationary subject. You may be at a medium shot of a speaker discussing a book, for example, and you tilt down from the speaker's face to the book on a table or in his or her hand. Like the other shots mentioned above, do not tilt too fast or too slowly.

More sophisticated productions will include *trucking* and *dollying* shots. It is very unlikely that you will use these unless you have a dolly, a tripod with wheels. If you do, try to follow action such as the presenter walking from side to side or front to back in the scene.

POST PRODUCTION

This step includes editing or re-shooting if necessary. Hopefully, your good planning and rehearsal yielded a good product which does not need editing. But what if you do need to get out some glitches in the video? Computers can make the editing process simple. There are many software programs that help you make edit decision lists (EDL) and will control two or more pieces of equipment using various editing protocols. Due to new compression techniques, you can store video clips on a computer hard disk, edit the clips and save them as a computer file. Unfortunately, most programs are crude, allowing for only a few minutes of storage, and poor quality output. Take heart, however, new technology is here with new compression techniques that will allow you to store and digitally edit one or more hours of video and digital audio on large hard disks. Editing software is simple, user friendly, and will enable the clips to be assembled into exciting video in about one-tenth the time of manual editing. You edit everything on the computer, store it as a file, and record tapes directly from the computer. Thus eliminating the generational image loss inherent in today's mechanical methods. The new full motion systems are very expensive, being purchased by commercial production companies to replace their aging mechanical systems. In a few years, however, these systems will become affordable for most school systems and businesses.

In reality, most schools and businesses do not have access to such computer editing systems. So we will focus on current mechanical methods.

First of all, you need at least two video machines. One will be the playback machine, the other one records. You also need a blank tape to make the edited recording. The easiest way to edit is to use the pause buttons on the machines or their remote controls.

1. Connect the two machines together using video dubbing cables, readily available at electronics or photo stores. Plug the cables into the video and audio "out" holes in the back of the play machine. Plug the other end of the cables into the video and audio "in" connections on the record machine. These connections will often be labeled "Line In" or Line Out." It is easy to remember, the signal goes out of the play machine into the record machine.

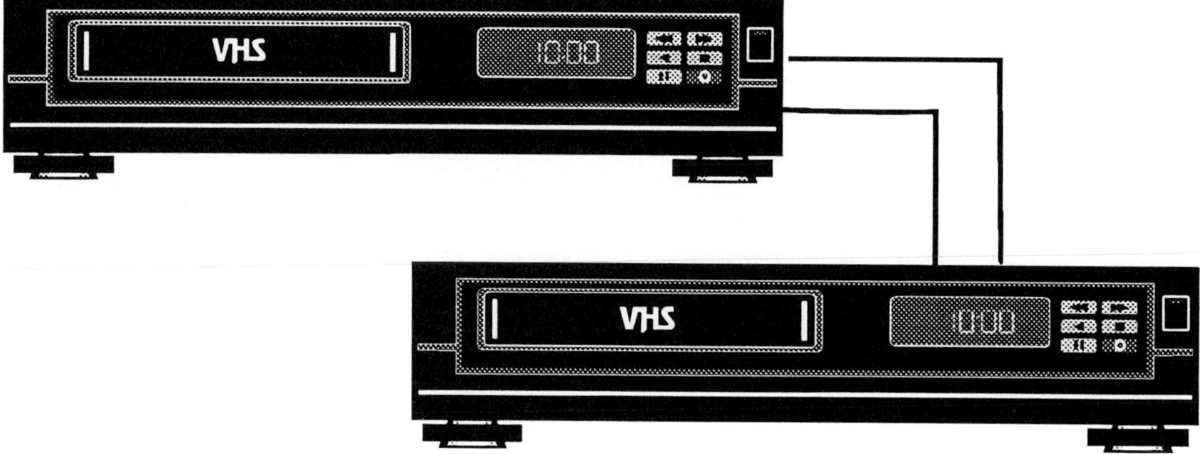

48

2. Start the record machine first and record about 15 seconds of black.

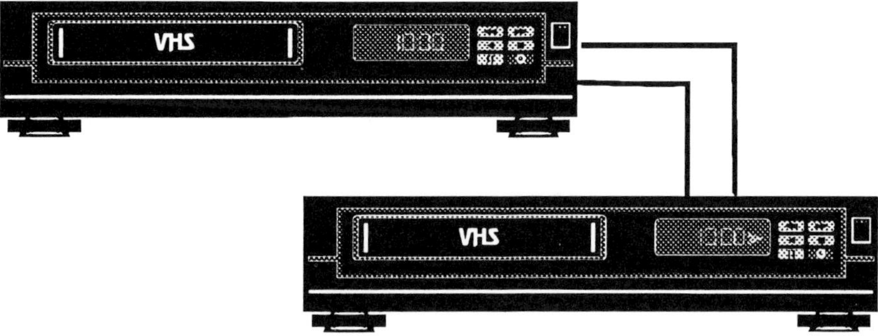

3. Start the playback machine; the program is now being recorded onto another tape.

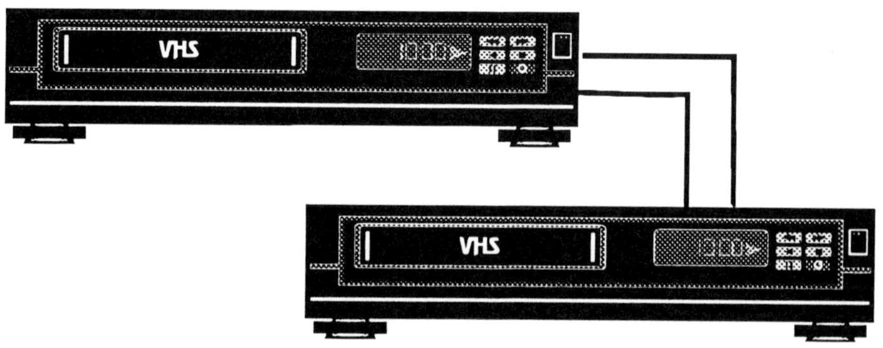

4. When you get to the glitch on the program, pause the record machine.

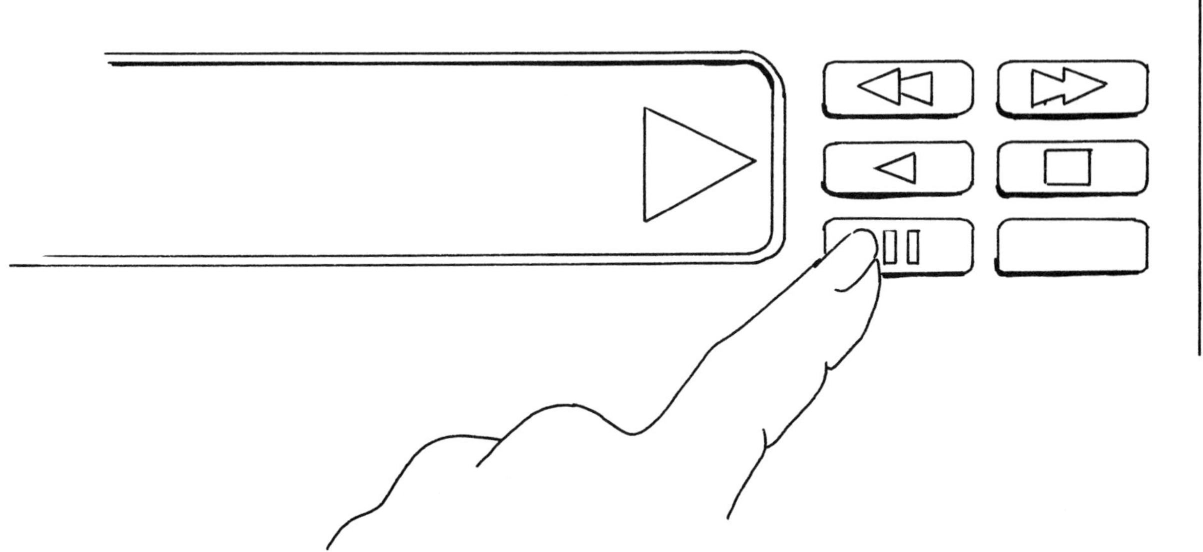

5. Release the pause button when the glitch passes. Do this for each error you want to eliminate. It is important to use the pause function instead of the stop/start buttons because using" pause" makes a smoother transition.

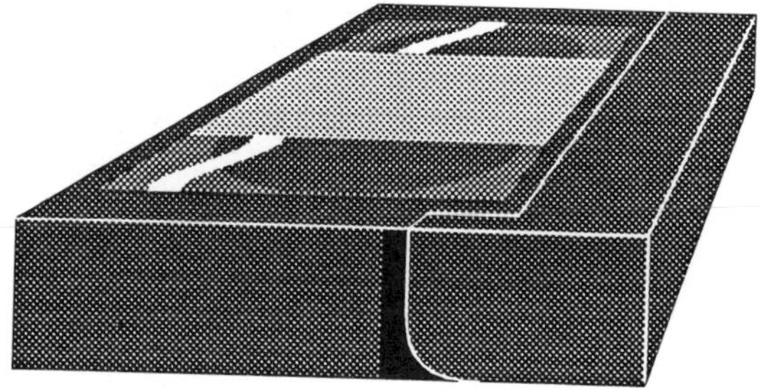

You have just accomplished rudimentary assembly editing. Most of the time it is not necessary to be very accurate, but if you need frame accuracy, take the master to a professional editing suite and pay the pros to do it. Frame accurate editing equipment costs thousands of dollars and most schools and businesses do not have the machines. This equipment usually consists of the recorders, a time base corrector, an edit controller, and other items to keep the video signal clean and clear, or add special effects such as wipes and fades.

The newly edited tape is another generation. Remember, the more generations you go down, the worse the picture gets. Avoid editing by good planning and rehearsal.

If you like the final product, you are ready to show it to an awaiting audience.

Part Two
LESSON PLANS

Teacher's Manual

This syllabus is based on a 14 or 15 week college semester course. It can be adjusted to fit any high school or college program.

GENERAL INFORMATION

CLASS ATTENDANCE: You are required to attend all scheduled classes, and any scheduled workshops. A Saturday workshop, if necessary, will replace the regular class meeting. Arrange with the instructor in advance, any time you need to make-up if you must miss a scheduled class or workshop. You receive a grade of "F" for every unexcused absence. These grades are included as class participation and factored into the final grade.

GRADES: The following are the grades you will receive for this course:

1. Class participation - this is based on how well you use class time to produce projects.

2. Class projects, and their design documents:

    a. teaching picture, dry mounted and laminated

    b. accordion fold or flip chart

    c. felt or bulletin board

    d. overhead transparency, with overlays

    e. opaque projection

    f. audio cassette tape (team)

    g. slide/tape program, 2-3 minutes (team)

    h. video program, :30 seconds to 5 minutes (team)

3. Team grades are given for each appropriate team project. Everyone on the team receives the same grade.

4. The final exam consists of 50 definitions and media selection criteria. The exam is included as a project grade.

DESIGN DOCUMENTS are required for each project. This is the term for the media plan, which includes a lesson plan. You are expected to be familiar with writing behavioral objectives and lesson plans. We will review these techniques in the class on media planning. You do not have to type the design documents unless you want to.

INCOMPLETE is not given. All projects must be turned in on time. Late projects drop one letter grade per class period late. You will get a grade of "F" for any project not turned in by the last class session.

SCOPE AND SEQUENCE

THE COURSE DIVIDES INTO FOUR UNITS, 15 CLASSES

CLASS ONE: Course introduction and requirements.

CLASS TWO, UNIT ONE, Lesson one: Introduction to media design and production.

CLASS THREE, UNIT ONE, Lesson two: Teaching pictures, dry mounting, and lamination.

CLASS FOUR, UNIT ONE, Lesson three: Opaque projections, and large pictures.

CLASS FIVE, UNIT ONE, Lesson four: Combining teaching pictures, felt boards.

CLASS SIX, UNIT TWO, Lesson one: Overhead transparency.

CLASS SEVEN, UNIT TWO, Lesson two: Audio production

CLASS EIGHT, UNIT THREE, Lesson one: Photographic media; filmstrips, slide programs, 8mm and 16mm movies.

CLASS NINE, UNIT THREE, Lesson two: Continuation of class eight.

CLASS TEN, UNIT FOUR, Lesson one: Videotape production.

CLASS ELEVEN, UNIT FOUR, Lesson two: Videotape production, continued.

CLASS TWELVE, UNIT FOUR, Lesson three: Videotape production, continued.

EXTRA CREDIT WORKSHOP: Television talent orientation

CLASS THIRTEEN, UNIT FOUR, Lesson four: Videotape production, continued.

CLASS FOURTEEN: FINAL EXAM

CLASS FIFTEEN: COURSE EVALUATION (This class can be eliminated in 14 week programs)

EQUIPMENT NEEDED TO ADEQUATELY COMPLETE THIS COURSE

Dry Mount Press	Slide Projector
Tacking Iron	Opaque Projector
Thermafax Machine	Video Camera
Audio Tape Recorders	35mm Camera
Video Tape Recorders	Copy Stand
Slide Sync Unit	Caramate
Opaque Projector	Video Monitor
Overhead Projector	Filmstrip Projector
Microphones	Felt Board
Easel	Tripod
Light Meter	Lights
16 mm movie projector	8mm movie projector

Provide the necessary accessories to your students including cables, seal lamin, MT-5 mounting tissue, rubber cement, poster board for demonstrations, marking pens, etc. Students must provide film, transparency film, and other items as needed.

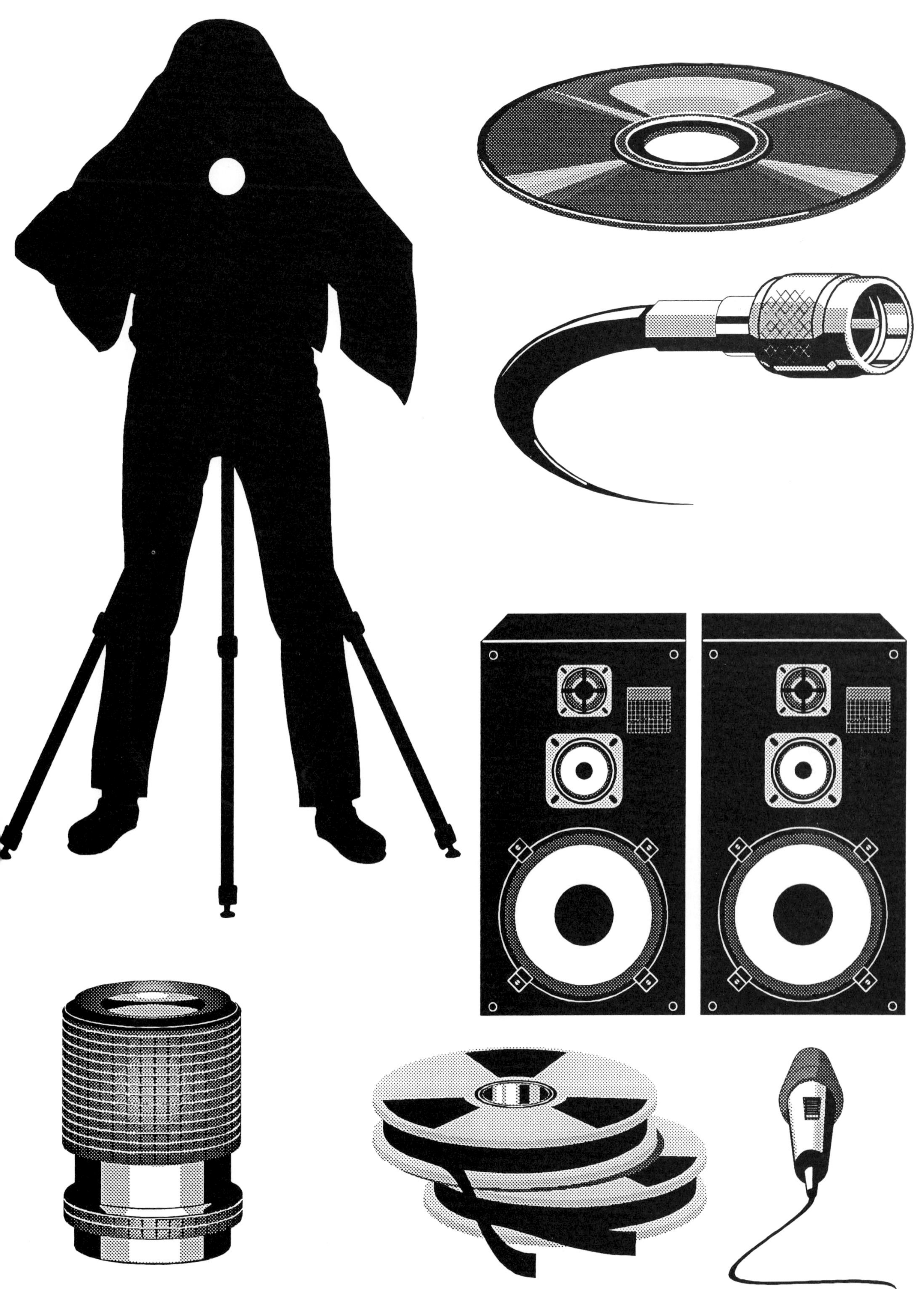

Unit One
Basics, and Simple Media

Lesson One
Lesson Two
Lesson Three
Lesson Four

UNIT ONE
LESSON ONE

Lesson Plan

GOAL: To give the class an overview of media methods, selection, and production.

BEHAVIORAL OBJECTIVES:

1. Given the lecture and handout materials, the student will define the term media. Acceptable performance consists of the students verbally repeating the definition to the instructor.

2. Given the lecture and handout materials, the student will identify the appropriate media for use in a certain classroom situation. Acceptable performance consists of the students verbally repeating the answer to the instructor. As an example, the student should know that 8mm movie production and selection is not appropriate for a class where the student needs immediate feedback.

3. Given examples, the student will identify the INDOC terms. Acceptable performance consists of the student saying the terms *Identify, Name, Describe, Order*, and *Construct*.

4. Given examples, the student will construct a behavioral objective. Acceptable performance consists of the student ordering the three parts; *conditions, behavior,* and performance level.

5. Given examples, the student will construct an affective domain objective.

6. Given examples and review, the student will describe media task analysis.

7. Given examples, the student will describe analysis of target population. Acceptable performance consists of adequate analysis of target audience's reading level, grade level, and social circumstances.

8. Given the previous instruction, the student will construct media design documents. Acceptable performance consists of the student combining task analysis, analysis of target population, behavioral and affective domain objectives into one plan.

AFFECTIVE DOMAIN OBJECTIVES:

1. The student will appreciate the value of media in the classroom.

2. The student will understand the educational differences between the various media.

3. The student will understand the necessity for proper planning and design of media, before production begins.

CLASSROOM ACTIVITIES:

1. lecture

2. media demonstrations

3. students practice writing objectives, selecting media, and writing design documents

REQUIRED MATERIALS: Students do not need any special materials other than a notebook, and the class handouts.

FOLLOW-UP ACTIVITIES:

1. Students bring 2 or 3 tear sheets (from magazines or wherever they can find them) to the next class for mounting.

2. Students will prepare design documents for the teaching pictures to be mounted and laminated in the next class.

Lesson Plan

GOAL: To take very simple pictures from posters, magazines, etc., and make useful instructional images, or aids.

BEHAVIORAL OBJECTIVES:

1. Given selection criteria, the student will identify good visuals for use as classroom teaching pictures. Acceptable performance consists of the student choosing the best 2 or 3 pictures from the selection brought to class.

2. Given a ruler, an X-acto knife, and cutting board, the student will construct a properly trimmed visual. Acceptable performance consists of using the metal edge of the ruler as guide, and cutting no more than 1/8 of an inch evenly across all four sides of the visual.

3. Given the trimmed visual, rubber cement, cutting board or magazine, and poster board as mounting material, the student will construct a mounted teaching picture. Acceptable performance consists of completing the following steps in succession:

    a. register the visual on the poster board by placing pencil marks on the opposite corners

    b. place rubber cement on one-half of the poster board

    c. place rubber cement on one-half of the visual

    d. place the cemented half of the visual on the cemented half of the poster board a press lightly

e. place rubber cement on the other half of the poster board

f. place rubber cement on the remaining half of the visual

g. lightly press the visual to the poster board

h. use the ruler to smooth out the visual on the poster board

i. rub-off the excess rubber cement with a clean finger

To receive a grade of "C" on this project, the visual must be neatly trimmed, **centered,** with no glue lumps, and no pencil or other dirt smears. Design documents must also accompany the mounted visual.

4. Given a visual, MT-5 mounting tissue, tacking iron, dry mount press, **and** weight, the student will construct a dry mounted teaching picture. Acceptable performance consists of the student completing the following steps in **sequence:**

a. select the appropriate visual

b. rough cut a piece of MT-5, and tack to the back of the visual **with the** tacking iron

c. trim the edges of the visual with the ruler and X-acto knife in the **same** manner as for the wet mount listed above

d. register the visual onto poster board using pencil marks on **opposite** corners of the visual

e. tack opposite ends of the loose MT-5 tissue within the registration marks

f. turn on dry mount press to 225 degrees to pre-heat

g. place semi-mounted visual into press and cook for about two **minutes**

h. remove from press and place mounted visual immediately under weight until cool (about 10 minutes)

To receive a grade of "C" on this mount, the visual must be centered, with no curl in the board, no bubbles from the mounting tissue, no excess tissue on the edges of the visual, and no pencil smears. Design documents are also required. It is recommended to pre-cook the poster board before mounting a visual, to remove excess water. This helps reduce curling when the visual cools. Students who do this procedure and meet the above criteria will receive at least a "B" project grade.

5. Given a third, mounted visual and some seal lamin laminating material, the student will construct a mounted and laminated teaching picture. Acceptable performance consists of the student completing the following steps in sequence:

a. cut an appropriate size of seal lamin from the roll with an X-acto knife

b. place mounted visual on top of seal

c. fold seal over either top and bottom, or sides of visual

d. tack seal to back of visual

e. place visual in an envelope made from newsprint, to protect the inside of the press from the seal sticking to the felt

f. place visual into dry mount press, and cook for about 2 minutes at 180 degrees

g. remove laminated visual from press and immediately place under weight for about 15 minutes

h. remove visual from under weight when cool

i. trim excess seal from all sides of the visual with straight edge and X-acto knife

j. re-cook visual if there are bubbles, or if the lamination appears cloudy

To receive a "C" grade on this project, the visual must not have bubbles, or be curled. Edges must be neatly trimmed, and design documents accompany the visual.

AFFECTIVE DOMAIN OBJECTIVES:

1. the student will appreciate the instructional value of a single, mounted teaching picture

2. the student will develop clean, neat, and detailed production habits

REQUIRED MATERIALS:

1. 3-5 tear sheet visuals

2. two pieces of 20" x 28" poster board

3. miscellaneous items such as pencils, eraser, ruler, etc

CLASSROOM ACTIVITIES: A demonstration by the instructor and hands-on construction by the students.

FOLLOW-UP ACTIVITIES: Students will keep these mounted visuals for use in the next two classes.

UNIT ONE
LESSON THREE

Lesson Plan

GOAL: To show students what can be done to enhance classroom learning using very large, poster size, and custom visuals taken from books or objects.

BEHAVIORAL OBJECTIVES:

1. Given an opaque projector, book (or magazine, etc.), drawing materials, and poster board, the student will construct a large copy of a visual chosen from the opaque source. Acceptable performance consists of the student completing the following steps in sequence:

    a. tape a large (over 11 x 14" size) piece of poster board onto a wall

    b. place book into opaque projector

    c. adjust projector or board height to fill board with projected image

    d. focus opaque projector

    e. re-adjust board or projector so that focused image fills entire board

    f. lightly trace projected image on the poster board

    g. remove board from wall and turn off projector lamp

2. Given the traced visual, the student will construct the final visual. Acceptable performance consists of the student coloring in the traced lines to his or her satisfaction.

To earn a grade of "C" on this project, the visual must be neatly traced, and colored, and fit to the design documents.

AFFECTIVE DOMAIN OBJECTIVE: The student will understand that he or she is not limited in size, or source, of possible teaching pictures.

CLASSROOM ACTIVITIES: A demonstration is followed by hands-on practice by the students.

REQUIRED MATERIALS:

    1. large piece of poster board

    2. drawing materials

    3. a book or other source of visual to be traced

    4. colored markers, or black markers if no color is desired

FOLLOW-UP ACTIVITIES:

    1. students will bring the completed visuals to the next class

    2. students will think of a class unit where the combination of these visuals can be used

UNIT ONE
LESSON FOUR

Lesson Plan

GOAL: To show the students how they can combine the products made in the previous lessons into a simple "multi-media" product, and to show an alternate way to display cut-out teaching pictures.

BEHAVIORAL OBJECTIVES:

1. Given the visuals from the previous classes, and other new visuals, the student will construct an accordion fold. Acceptable performance consists of the student neatly taping two or more mounted visuals to form an accordion, which can be opened one visual at a time to achieve mastery of specific objectives.

2. Given individual cut-outs of visuals, the student will construct a simple sequence of action on a felt board. Acceptable performance consists of the student completing the following steps in sequence:

   a. cut-out small pieces of sandpaper

   b. glue one or more pieces of sandpaper to the backs of the cut-out visuals

   c. place the visuals on the felt board in the sequence outlined in the design documents

To receive a grade of "C" on both these projects, the visuals have to be neatly trimmed. Also, the student will present the accordion fold, and felt board lessons to the class, based on the design documents.

AFFECTIVE DOMAIN OBJECTIVES:

1. The student will understand how to combine simple media into more complicated media.

2. The student will know the value of sequential visual presentations.

3. The student will appreciate the use of inexpensive, everyday materials to produce educational products.

CLASSROOM ACTIVITIES:

1. demonstration by instructor

2. hands-on practice

3. students present brief lesson using the products they made in class

REQUIRED MATERIALS:

1. new visuals

2. sandpaper

3. glue

4. masking tape

5. felt board

6. any additional items the individual students need for their presentations

FOLLOW-UP ACTIVITIES: Students bring a photocopy of a picture, chart, etc, 8 1/2 by 11 " to the next class.

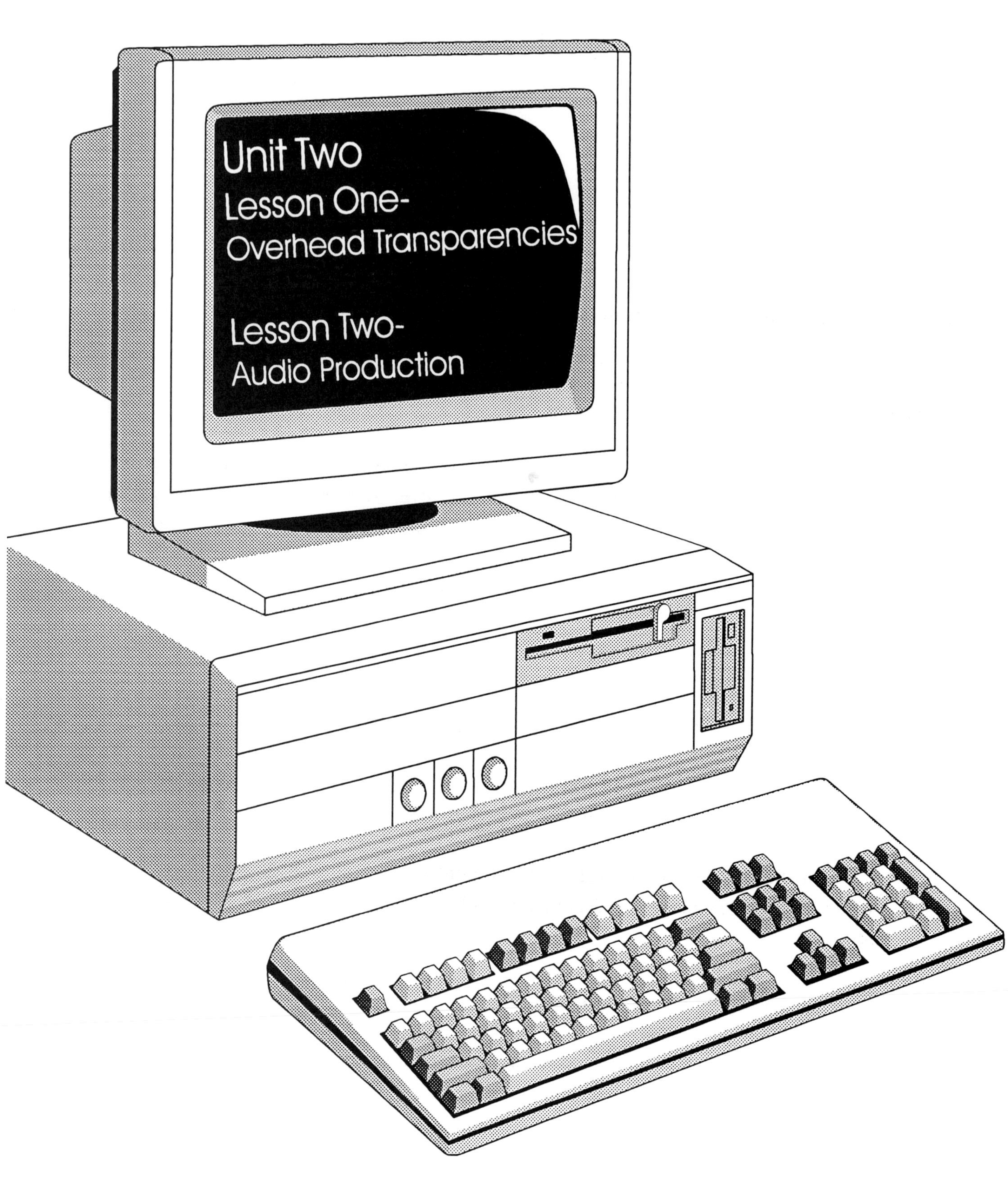

Unit Two
Lesson One-
Overhead Transparencies

Lesson Two-
Audio Production

Lesson Plan

GOAL: To show students two simple and fast ways to make overhead transparencies.

BEHAVIORAL OBJECTIVES:

1. Given a thermafax machine, transparency film, and pre-selected photocopy of an original visual, the student will construct an overhead transparency. Acceptable performance consists of the student completing the following steps in sequence:

   a. set heat control on thermafax machine to desired darkness level

   b. select desired color transparency film

   c. place original visual in the film packet as directed by the manufactures instructions on the box

   d. run the film packet through the machine

2. Given the finished transparency, the student will mount the final product. Acceptable performance consists of the student completing the following steps in sequence:

   a. center the visual in the mount

   b. tape the centered visual to the back of the mount

   c. title the mount as needed

3. Given a photocopy machine, transparency film, and original visual, the student will construct an overhead transparency. Acceptable performance consists of completing the following steps in sequence:

    a. load the copy machine with the appropriate type of transparency film

    b. make a copy of the original as would be done for any normal page

    c. mount the finished transparency as described in objective 2

4. Given the mount, and two or three transparencies, the student will construct an overlay transparency. Acceptable performance consists of completing the following steps in sequence:

    a. center and place the first transparency to appear on the screen in the mount

    b. tape all sides of this first transparency to the back of the mount,so that it forms the base

    c. tape the second transparency to one side of the back of the mount so that it forms a movable hinge

    d. tape the third transparency to another side of the mount in the same manner as "c" above

5. Given the finished overlay transparency, the student will describe the project to the class. Acceptable performance consists of the student teaching the objectives stated in the overlay design documents.

To receive a grade of "C" on these transparency projects, the following technical criteria must be met:

    1. the image on the transparency must not be too dark, or too light

2. any text on the transparency must be readable when projected onto the screen

3. no dirt spots on the transparency

4. no mounting tape should overflow onto the projected image

5. overlay tape hinges must be flexible to allow for easy flipping

AFFECTIVE DOMAIN OBJECTIVES:

1. the student will understand and appreciate how simple it is to make a transparency

2. the student will know how to combine single transparencies into overlays

3. the student will understand when transparencies are appropriate for instructions, and not overuse them

CLASSROOM ACTIVITIES: Instructor demonstrations followed by hands-on **practice**, and teaching using the overlays

REQUIRED MATERIALS: Students must have original source materials for visuals

FOLLOW-UP ACTIVITIES: None

UNIT TWO
LESSON TWO

Lesson Plan

GOAL: To introduce basic sound recording techniques

BEHAVIORAL OBJECTIVE: Given a tape recorder, tape, and script, the student will construct an instructional audio tape on the subject of their choice. Acceptable performance consists of producing a clearly audible cassette program, not to exceed 5 minutes in length.

AFFECTIVE DOMAIN OBJECTIVE: The student will appreciate the strengths and limits of stand-alone audio programs.

CLASSROOM ACTIVITIES:

   1. lecture and demonstration

   2. hands-on recording and script writing

REQUIRED MATERIALS: Students should bring a blank 30 or 60 minute cassette tape.

FOLLOW-UP ACTIVITIES: This tape will be used in the lesson on slide/tape production. Students should think about an appropriate script.

Unit Three

Lesson One
Slides & Movies

Lesson Two
Production

UNIT THREE
LESSON ONE

Lesson Plan

GOAL: To introduce the class to the photographic media, and start them planning for a slide/tape program.

BEHAVIORAL OBJECTIVES:

1. Given a sample filmstrip, the student will describe its proper use in the classroom to include advantages and disadvantages. Acceptable performance consists of the student stating that filmstrips are inexpensive, but hard to update, and should be used for individual or small groups due to equipment limitations.

2. Given a sample 16mm movie, the student will describe its proper use in the classroom, to include advantages and disadvantages. Acceptable performance consists of the student's description to include equipment limitations, image quality, out of date information, out of date production, and entertainment value.

3. Given a sample super 8mm movie, the student will describe its proper use and limitations, if any. Acceptable performance consists of a response including inconvenience of sound, availability of hardware, the time and expense of film processing, and overall image quality.

4. Given samples of still photographs, the student will describe how to incorporate this medium into the instruction. Acceptable performance will vary due to the possibility of creative responses from the student.

5. Given a sample slide/tape program, the student will describe its proper use in classroom instruction to include advantages and disadvantages. Acceptable

performance consists of mentioning availability of equipment, image quality, ease of updating, relative low cost to produce, relative ease of production, and task isolation and analysis.

6. Given the sample slide program, the student will construct design documents for their production. This may be completed outside of class.

7. Given a camera, the student will take photographs, if necessary, for his or her upcoming program.

8. Given an audio recorder, the student will construct an audio tape to be used with his or her slide program.

AFFECTIVE DOMAIN OBJECTIVE: The student will understand the uses, and limitations of the photographic media for classroom instruction.

CLASSROOM ACTIVITIES:

1. lecture

2. demonstration of samples

3. student preparation of design documents, photography, and audio for the next class

REQUIRED MATERIALS: Students need a roll of film, and cassette tape.

FOLLOW-UP ACTIVITIES: Students will prepare a slide/tape presentation in the next class.

UNIT THREE
LESSON TWO

Lesson Plan

GOAL: To produce a short slide/tape program.

BEHAVIORAL OBJECTIVES:

1. Given the design documents, the student will construct a script.

2. Given processed slides, the student will order them in the slide tray. Acceptable performance consists of the order correctly following the task analysis and behavioral objectives of the script.

3. Given the audio tape, the student will synchronize the slides to the tape. Acceptable performance consists of the student accurately following the script, and manually putting the pulse tone after the appropriate slide advance.

To receive a grade of "C" on this project, the student must teach the rest of the class a short unit using the slide program.

AFFECTIVE DOMAIN OBJECTIVES:

1. The student will appreciate the complexities, and value, of developing a slide/tape instructional program.

2. The student will understand how the slide/tape media fit into the overall classroom instruction.

CLASSROOM ACTIVITIES:

    1. lecture and demonstration by instructor

    2. hands-on practice by the students

    3. students teach the rest of the class using their programs

REQUIRED MATERIALS: Same as for the previous class.

FOLLOW-UP ACTIVITIES: None

Unit Four
Videotape Production

Lesson One
Lesson Two
Lesson Three
Lesson Four

Lesson Plan

GOAL: To introduce the class to television production, and planning.

BEHAVIORAL OBJECTIVES:

1. Given a lecture and class discussion, the student will form a production team with two or three other classmates (depending on the class size).

2. Given the production team, the student will describe an idea for a short video production.

3. Given a lecture and demonstration, the student team will name an appropriate videotape format for their production. Acceptable performance will consist of the group selecting either 3/4 ", VHS, Beta, or 8mm format for their project.

4. Given the team idea, the production team will construct appropriate design documents.

5. Given the design documents, the production team will construct a script. Acceptable performance consist of the script adhering to the behavioral objectives, and concepts in the design documents.

6. Given the script, the production team will construct a storyboard. Acceptable performance consists of the storyboard being a visual representation of the script. They may produce more than one storyboard showing a variety of visual concepts for the script.

7. Given the script, and story board, the team will describe the use of talent in their production.

AFFECTIVE DOMAIN OBJECTIVES:

1. The student will appreciate the amount of planning and organization required for television production.

2. The student will understand the limitations of television production in a school situation, specifically the lack of sophisticated equipment, and constraints of taping in a classroom with large groups of inexperienced students.

3. The student will understand the influence of commercial television on children, and exploit that influence as motivation for student participation in classroom production.

4. The student will appreciate the value and limitations of the available video tape formats.

CLASSROOM ACTIVITIES:

1. lecture and demonstration of video formats by the instructor

2. lecture and samples of scripts and storyboards

3. production team discussions and practical work on the design documents, scripts, and storyboards

4. additional group planning for the production

REQUIRED MATERIALS: Students just need the basic pencil, paper, etc. The school provides blank script sheets and poster board.

FOLLOW-UP ACTIVITIES: Students should read relevant materials cited in the bibliography (a handout at the beginning of the course) on television production, and have their production plan finalized before the next class.

Lesson Plan

GOAL: To give students basic video production skills, including camera operation and lighting.

BEHAVIORAL OBJECTIVES:

1. Given a 3/4" camera, VHS and Beta cameras, and an 8mm video camera, the student will identify the differences in size, quality, and controls. Acceptable performance consists of the student stating that the white balance, focus, iris setting, zoom, and power controls on the 3/4" camera are manually operated, whereas the others have auto controls.

2. Given a VHS camcorder and tripod, the student will mount the camera on the tripod. Acceptable performance consists of the student unlocking the legs, then locking them into place, screwing the camera into the pod, and setting the elevation to a comfortable eye level.

3. Given the tripod and camera, the student will focus an image. Acceptable performance consists of a sharp image, front to back, as appears on the monitor.

4. Given the tripod and camera, the student will zoom into an object. Acceptable performance consists of a smooth transition from a medium shot to a close-up.

5. Given the camera and tripod, the student will tilt on the object. Acceptable performance consists of a smooth movement from top to bottom, and bottom to top of the object.

6. Given the camera and tripod, the student will pan an object. Acceptable performance consists of a smooth movement from left to right, and right to left of the object.

7. Given the camera, tripod, and moving object, the student will follow the person's movement. Acceptable performance consists of the moving object being centered in the frame.

8. Given the camera only, the student will complete the above techniques, using only shoulder support. Acceptable performance consists of the student maintaining a steady image while hand holding the camera.

9. Given the camcorder, the student will load the blank video tape.

10. Given the camcorder, the student will unload a used video tape.

11. Given the practice above, the student will be able to describe the basic points of framing and composition. Acceptable performance consists of the student stating, or showing by example, how to fill the frame with an image so that the top of a head is about one inch from the top of the monitor screen.

12. Given the previous practice, the student will identify the following types of shots, and their uses:

    a. long shot

    b. medium shot

    c. close-up

    d. extreme close-up

Acceptable performance consists of the student stating that the LS is used to establish a scene, and is at wide angle to include all major characters or places. MS are more tightly framed and isolate one or more of the characters or objects to show visual relationships. CU are used to isolate one character speaking, or reacting to the previous shot. XCU show only a part of a face, or object, and is rarely used except to show writing or for a special effect.

13. Given the three types of video tape recorders, the student will load, play, cue, rewind, and eject a tape.

AFFECTIVE DOMAIN OBJECTIVES:

1. The student will understand how easy it is to video tape activity in the classroom.

2. At the same time, the student will understand the complexities of video tape recording.

3. The student will appreciate the value of video tape production in the classroom.

CLASSROOM ACTIVITIES:

1. lecture and demonstration by the instructor

2. practice of the techniques by the students

REQUIRED MATERIALS: No special materials are required by the students.

FOLLOW-UP ACTIVITIES: Students may practice on their own, and prepare to shoot their scripts during the next two classes.

Lesson Plan

GOAL: To let the students produce their own educational video program.

BEHAVIORAL OBJECTIVE: Given the equipment and previous instruction, the student will construct, with the production team, a short (5 minutes or less) video program. Acceptable performance consists of the group teaching the rest of the class a brief unit which incorporates the video. Production techniques must meet the same criteria as described in the previous lessons.

AFFECTIVE DOMAIN OBJECTIVE: The student will enjoy producing television programs with his or her fellow students.

CLASSROOM ACTIVITIES: The students are involved in independent production, with the instructor available as a resource person.

REQUIRED MATERIALS: Students bring any materials necessary for their productions. The school provides blank tape and cameras.

FOLLOW-UP ACTIVITIES: Students continue production into the next class.

FINAL EXAM

GOAL: To test the students knowledge of terminology.

BEHAVIORAL OBJECTIVE: Given a written test, the student will identify 50 media terms. Acceptable performance consists of the student correctly identifying 35 of the 50 terms. The grade scale is as follows:

A = 90 to 100%

B = 80 to 89%

C = 70 to 79%

D = 60 to 69%

F = 0 to 59%

This final exam counts as one project grade.

AFFECTIVE DOMAIN OBJECTIVES: None

CLASSROOM ACTIVITIES:

    1. students take a written test

    2. instructor evaluates video tapes made in previous lesson

REQUIRED MATERIALS: None

FOLLOW-UP ACTIVITIES: None

Index & Bibliography

Bibliography

This bibliography is a sampling of other books on media topics. Although none were used as sources for my research, you may want to look at some of these for additional ideas and techniques. Most are still in print. The older ones are still very useful, especially in the area of script writing.

General Topics

AV Marketplace. New York: Bowker, 1969-

Allen, James A. The Audiovisual Handbook: How to Save Money on AV Rentals. Atlanta: Allen Media Services, 1993.

Branyan-Broadbent, Brenda and Wood, R. Kent. Educational Media and Technology Yearbook. Englewood, CO: Libraries Unlimited, 1991.

Bullough, Robert V. Display Boards, Duane, James E. ed. (The Instructional Media Library, vol. 3) Englewood Cliffs, NJ: Educational Technology Publications, 1981.

__________ Multi-Image Media. Duane, James E. ed. (The Instructional Media Library, vol. 9) Englewood Cliffs, NJ: Educational Technology Publications, 1981.

Commins, Elaine. Bloomin' Bulletin Boards. Atlanta: Humanics Ltd., 1992.

Darnton, P. Audio Techniques in Training. (The Training Technology Programme Series) Pearl River, NY: Parthenon Pub., 1987.

Display: A Handbook of Bulletin Board Ideas. (The Spice Series). Atlanta: Education Serv., 1975.

Dungey, Joan M. Interactive Bulletin Boards as Teaching Tools. Washington, DC: National Education Association, 1989.

Ellington, Henry. Producing Teaching Materials: A Handbook for Teachers and Trainers, 2nd Edition. East Brunswick, NJ: Nichols Pubs., 1993.

Kenyon, N. and Nightingale, C. Audiovisual Telecommunications. New York: Van Nostrand Reinhold, 1992.

Kostelanetz, Richard. <u>Audio Writing</u>. New York: Archae Editions, 1984.

Morse, Carmel L. <u>Audio-Visual Primer</u>. Dayton: Backwoods Pubns., 1983.

Parker, Norton S. <u>Audiovisual Script Writing</u>. New Brunswick: Rutgers University Press, 1974.

Peace, Jacquelyn and Peterson, Carol A. <u>Complete Audiovisual Guide for Teachers and Media Specialists</u>. New York: Prentice-Hall, 1989.

Perez, Jeannine. <u>Bulletin Board Basics, Hands-On Science</u>. Bridgeport: First Teacher Press, 1991.

Satterthwaite, Les L. <u>Instructional Media: Materials, Production and Utilization</u>. Dubuque: Kendall/Hunt, 1991.

Schwier, Richard A. and Misanchuk, Earl R. <u>Interactive Multimedia Instruction</u>. Englewood Cliffs, NJ: Educational Technology Publications, 1993.

Slawson, Ron. <u>Multi-Image Slide-Tape Programs</u>. Englewood, CO: Libraries Unlimited, 1988.

Swain, Dwight V. <u>Scripting for Video and Audiovisual Media</u>. Boston: Focal Press, 1981.

Thorpe, R. <u>Projected Still Images in Training</u> (The Training Technology Programme Series, Vol. 10). Atlanta: Parthenon Pub., 1987.

Volker and Simonson. <u>Media for Teachers,</u> 5th Edition. Dubuque: Kendall/Hunt, 1989.

Wileman, Ralph E. <u>Visual Communicating</u>. Englewood Cliffs, NJ: Educational Technology Publications, 1993.

Video Production

Bensinger, Charles. <u>Video Production Guide</u>. Sante Fe: Timewindow Publications, 1983.

Bernard, Robert. <u>Practical Videography: Field Systems</u>. Boston: Focal Press, 1992.

Blyth-Lor, Robin. <u>Captions and Graphics for Low Cost Video</u>. Boston: Focal Press, 1992.

Brown, Blain. <u>Filmmaker's Pocket Reference</u>. Boston: Focal Press, 1993.

Brown, Michael. <u>Desktop Video Production</u>. Blue Ridge Summit, PA: TAB Books, 1990.

Carson, Dina. <u>Easy and Affordable Video... Even If You Don't Own a Camera</u>. Boulder, CO: Iron Gate Publishing, 1992.

Caruso, James R. <u>Video Lighting and Special Effects</u>. New York: Prentice/Hall, 1991.

DeLuca, Stuart. <u>Instructional Video</u>. Boston: Focal Press, 1990.

Dennison, Dell, et. al. <u>Producing a First-Class Video for Your Business: Work with Professionals or Do It Yourself.</u> Bellingham, WA: ISC Press, 1992.

Dizazzo, Ray. <u>Directing Corporate Video</u>. Boston: Focal Press, 1993.

Eustace, Grant. <u>Writing for Corporate Video</u>. Boston: Focal Press, 1990.

Gayeski, Diane. <u>Corporate and Instructional Video</u>. New York: Prentice-Hall, 1991.

Hedgecoe, John. <u>John Hedgecoe's Complete Video Course: A Step-by-Step, Self-Instructional Guide to Making Great Videos</u>. New York: Simon and Schuster, 1989.